THE CHANGING FACE OF
CATHOLIC IRELAND

THE CHANGING FACE
OF
CATHOLIC IRELAND

EDITED BY

DESMOND FENNELL

Foreword by Karl Rahner, S.J.

GEOFFREY CHAPMAN
LONDON DUBLIN MELBOURNE 1968

Geoffrey Chapman Ltd
18 High Street, Wimbledon, London SW 19

Geoffrey Chapman (Ireland) Ltd
5-7 Main Street, Blackrock, County Dublin

Geoffrey Chapman Pty Ltd
44 Latrobe Street, Melbourne, Vic 3000, Australia

First published 1968

Much of the material in this book was first published in *Herder Correspondence* from November 1964 to January 1968. The publishers are grateful to the editor for permission to reprint.

This book is set in 11 on 12 pt Baskerville
Printed in Great Britain by
Clarke, Doble & Brendon Ltd, Cattedown, Plymouth

CONTENTS

In memory
of
HERBERT AUHOFER

FOREWORD by Karl Rahner, S.J.

The editor has asked me to contribute a short foreword. I find it hard to imagine that anything I might say would add to the value of this important book on the recent history of Catholic Ireland, all the more so since I am no expert on the subject. Nevertheless, I am glad to have this opportunity of saying to the Irish Catholic readers of this book that I believe their postconciliar Church can, and indeed will, have an important role to play in the universal Church, just as Catholic Ireland before the Council, through its loyalty in the faith, its abundance of priests, its missionary activity, and above all through its influence on the American Catholic Church, rendered important service to the Church as a whole.

I am regarded, oddly enough, especially in the English-speaking countries, as a leading exponent of the 'diaspora thesis' of the Church—the view that the Church of the future cannot expect to be anywhere in the world the Church of a homogeneously Christian society, but must count rather on being and remaining, sociologically speaking, a particular ideological group in a pluralistic society. Obviously, this thesis is not meant to indicate an ideal, but simply the probable course of things to come. It does not suggest that the Church should abandon the resolute courage of its commitment to bringing the Gospel to as many peoples and individuals as possible, that it should resign its mission to convert as many people as possible into baptized Christians and convinced members of the Church. Neither does it mean—and this I should like to say to my Irish brothers in the Church—that one must abandon in advance the resolve and the hope that Churches which are now almost identical with the society of a particular people will be carried over into the pluralistic world society of the future.

The thesis of the Church in the diaspora has never stated nor intended that the percentage of Church-affiliated Christians

7

either would be or should be the same in every country. The
diaspora in which the Church of the future will live is a mankind
which in spite of all its tragic divisions is growing together to a
certain unity. Within this diaspora of the world there may be, and
there should be, areas inhabited by large, coherent Christian
groups, each of them still more or less identical with a single
historic people. The Church of such a people will, of course, be
living in the diaspora for the simple reason that the people in
question, as a concrete part of a mankind that is growing to unity,
will be unable to shut themselves off in an 'insular' manner from
the life and the fortunes of that pluralistic world. Such a people,
still Christian and taking its churched Christianity with it into
that diaspora, has a mission to the world at large cut out for it
by these very facts. Perhaps we can no longer hope for such a
future for many peoples or Churches of peoples; but perhaps the
Poles, the Spaniards, and above all the Irish, are such peoples.

Such a Christian people has then the task both of preserving
what is native to it and of re-possessing this ancient, distinctive
heritage in a courageous intellectual tussle with the pluralistic
world culture in which it lives, so as to make its inherited
Christianity of an entire people into a leaven for the world at
large. This, as I see it, is Ireland's role. The Irish are not obliged
to take over, in a block deal, the theology and Church life of the
Continent, worked out as these have been in largely dechristianized
society; nor would it be right for them to do so. Rather must
they develop out of the unbroken strength of their own 'people's
Church' a theology of their own and their own postconciliar
Church life. Ireland has no call for an inferiority complex *vis-à-
vis* the Continent or for a permanent squint in that direction, as
if Church and theology were so provided there that, to have a
modern theology and a modern Church, one needed merely to
take them over intact. Of course, if the Irish are to fulfil their
role in the unified world of the future—by being clearly a Catholic people and by impinging as such in a missionary manner on
the entire world—their theology and their Church life must face
up to the situations and the questions posed by a world which is
by no means Christian only, but a diaspora in which the world
Church lives. In this respect, Continental theology and the life of

Europe as a whole can offer a certain assistance to Catholic Ireland in the fulfilment of its task.

If in Ireland there is no 'lost working class', if even in the cities ninety per cent of the people fill the churches on Sundays, if there are so many vocations to the priesthood that other countries can share in this rich blessing, if Ireland is still making a contribution to mission work abroad which is far beyond the average for the originally Christian countries—then this is proof sufficient that in Ireland the Church is still the Church of the people and not of a minority group in a pluralistic society. Clearly, this grace which has been given to the Irish must be preserved for the benefit of the entire Church. But it is not by clinging to the past in a reactionary manner but by winning a new future for the past, that this can be done. In Ireland as elsewhere there will be difficulties. These will arise, on the one hand, out of the growth at home of an industrial society based on rationalistic science and technology, on the other, out of the increasing contacts and exchanges with the life and thought of mankind as a whole. But for a Christian optimism these difficulties will occur merely to be overcome, and the hope that they will be overcome is well-founded: for the Irish are still a Christian people.

KARL RAHNER, S.J.

EDITOR'S NOTE

Except for the two leading articles reprinted on pages 13-15 all the articles reprinted here were the joint work of the *Herder Correspondence* team of researchers, writers and correspondents. They appeared in *Herder Correspondence* from September 1964 until January 1968. When pieces which first appeared singly, separated by months and even years, are brought together to form a book, certain minor adjustments are necessary in the interests of readability and consecutiveness. I have tried to make these adjustments. I have also re-written sentences here and there which seemed awkwardly phrased, deleted a few narrowly topical references and made a few corrections of fact which had been brought to my notice. But I have altered no evaluation or emphasis in the light of subsequent events. Insofar as some of the reports included here are directly contemporary chronicles, written under the impact of the events they record, I have let them retain this quality. In a Postscript I try to draw the various threads together and offer a personal view of the recent history and present situation of the Catholic Irish.

Inasmuch as there is no comprehensive account of modern Irish Catholicism available, this book serves to plug a yawning gap. When the subject is so large and the gap so yawning as in the present case, even an account such as this, which lays no claim to being definitive, must serve a useful purpose. If this book inspires more ambitious works, if it is quickly and effectively superseded, it will have served its purpose well. In the meantime it can claim to throw some general light where there is at present little more than patchy darkness.

DESMOND FENNELL

PRELUDE

On 17 March, from Buenos Aires to Dublin, from Tokyo to New York and Rangoon, the bells of 2,000 cathedrals and parish churches of St Patrick will toll with more than ordinary ardour. No one, least of all the Irish themselves, has yet come near to explaining the special mystery of the modern Irish Catholic people, so strangely repeating Israel in their fusion of nationality and religion and in their salvific dispersion from a small homeland to a worldwide diaspora. On the contrary, due precisely to their fusion of nationality and Catholic religion in an age when each was believed to excise men definitively from the common human lot, the specialness of the Irish has been a subject of sterile fascination for themselves and for others far too long. As a result they have been seen, and have seen themselves, whether for good or ill, as characterized by *difference* only and not by shared qualities of humanity and culture.

Once this dogma was established, the modern Irish people eluded understanding : for it was assumed *a priori*, by themselves and others, that they were not primarily human beings involved in modern Anglo-Saxon culture and late Tridentine Catholicism, but primarily, in an over-riding sort of way, 'Irish Catholics'— which could mean whatever you wanted it to mean!

The Catholic Irish of the last century or so have exemplified to an extreme degree the intellectual intramuralism and self-obsession, combined with a lack of humanist perspective, which we recently decried as *characteristic of Catholics in our time*. Small wonder then that, despite their reputation for talking, they have been unable to make coherent statements of any importance about this age or about Man. Despite their literary reputation, not one of them has yet written a single book of note about the English—to go no further!

[1] Leading Article, March 1967.

13

II[2]

Our Catholic renewal cannot take place in the dark. Good intentions and new theological insights are, even with the grace of God, utterly insufficient. We remain fumblers unless we see ourselves and the terrain of our lives completely and truly.

The members of each local, national church, and of those groups of local churches that are linked together by a shared language-culture, need to know the how and why and where of their specific historical situation and their specific cultural embodiment. Have English-speaking Catholics done this necessary mental work, or do they still cling to the habit which they acquired in their timid, appeasing days—their 'triumphalism' was more limited than they should have liked to admit!—of taking understanding of themselves, of their times, and of modern Anglo-Saxon culture on faith and by hearsay from the interpretative and evaluative establishments in their non-Catholic environment? Lashing out at defects does not necessarily indicate greater insight than complacency. It can indicate mere blind, futile fury—the fury of blind men being bruised by they know not what.

In the English language-culture, more completely than in any other outside Scandinavia, the Roman Catholic tradition was broken by the Reformation. In the other great cultures of western and central Europe, Catholics, continuing their Catholic cultural past, continued to shape, at least partially, the developing texture of language and ideas, of material and social culture. English-speaking Catholics virtually ceased to do this. For one thing, until the first quarter of the nineteenth century, their numbers were insignificant. For another, until the second quarter of the same century, whether they lived in Britain, Ireland or America, they were obliged by ruthless systems of penal laws and by the pressure of public opinion to lead an underground existence, socially and culturally. As a result, when modern English-speaking Catholicism began to grow numerically and geographically in the first half of the nineteenth century, it intruded into a powerful culture in which Catholics had had no

[2] Leading Article, March 1967.

place for nearly three centuries. Moreover, the rapid numerical growth which made Roman Catholicism once again into a powerful, if largely passive, presence in Anglo-Saxon culture was provided by people who had abandoned their own inherited language-cultures for this new one—in its nineteenth-century variants. (Only the few 'old' English-speaking Catholics and most of the converts did not share this particular cultural disadvantage.)

Not surprisingly then, this new participation of Catholics in the Anglo-Saxon language-culture has from the start been more marginal, passive, and uncreative than contemporary Catholic participation in any of the other major cultures of western and central Europe. Aware that they were suspect, happy to have regained the religious freedom long denied, lacking—the vast majority of them—an inherited language-culture which they could call their own, involved in a tremendous task of material and institutional construction that absorbed most of their energies, English-speaking Catholics were more than willing to accept the dominant culture as they found it. They submitted readily to a great deal of cultural brain-washing for the sake of peace, social acceptance, social power, material betterment, and the freedom to build their Church, their churches, and their schools.

What was the culture they adhered to? In the mid-nineteenth century the Liberal writer John Stuart Mill saw 'the two influences which have chiefly shaped the British character since the days of the Stuarts' as 'commercial money-getting business and religious Puritanism'. Besides 'commercial' and 'puritanical', a full characterization of the predominant cultural stream in nineteenth-century Britain, America, and Australia would have to include : democratic, liberal-utilitarian, anti-intellectual, philistine, isolationist in regard to continental European culture.

Leaving the ghetto mentality behind and starting from such basic facts, the self-understanding of English-speaking Catholics might well progress towards that critical and knowing view of themselves and of the world around them which would make their Christian renewal possible in the only medium in which history takes places—culture.

1

CHURCH AND STATE[1]

'It seems to me', said Judge Barra Ó Briain in Limerick Circuit Court on 21 May 1964, 'that forty years after this country has attained its independence, it should be possible to amend the law where for historical reasons it gives rise to grave problems of conscience. . . . Catholic citizens and judges, faced with these problems, have a right to ask that the law which requires amendment should be amended by those who create legislation.'

Judge Ó Briain was giving his decision in a case in which a woman pleaded guilty to bigamy by marrying in a Catholic church in Limerick, while the man she had married in an English registry office was still alive. The judge said that when she married the man in the Catholic church

'she was entirely correct to do so according to canon law despite flagrant disregard of civil law. There is a very serious conflict between civil and canon law in this country.'

The Dublin *Catholic Standard* of 19 June quoted the following comment by a 'distinguished Irish theologian' :

'The Constitution imposes monogamy, but does not define "marriage", which must be specifically determined by legislation. As a historical legacy, in this country we have an anomalous, indeed one might say scandalous, situation. A couple who, in the view of at least 95 per cent of the people, are validly married, can be publicly and legally branded as living in immorality. Their union is characterized as bigamous, and

[1] September 1964.

17

their children illegitimate. There is a general feeling that this situation should be remedied. This legal disability imposed on us Catholics is the more painful inasmuch as other citizens can go to England or across the border (to Northern Ireland) to obtain a divorce to contract a new marriage which the law accepts as valid.

'There is no need to alter the Constitution. I suggest that what we need is a new Nullity Act. In addition to codifying the natural law grounds for nullifying an alleged marriage (e.g. coercion), the measure should include a new provision : for abolishing the conflict between civil law and canon law. That means judicial acceptance and registration of a decree of nullity granted after investigation by the competent ecclesiastical court (e.g. the Rota). This concession to Catholics would not be of extended application, but it would put an end to painful incidents to which publicity has recently been given. Non-Catholics would in no way be penalized; they retain the curiously geographical facilities now available to them.'

It was not the first time that this kind of difficulty had arisen in the Republic of Ireland. The judge's dilemma can be understood only in the light of the unusual relationship between Church and State which exists in the Republic. The formal aspects of this relationship are adequately and concisely described in a book by a French diplomat and jurist, Jean Blanchard, which has recently appeared in English. The English title, *The Church in Contemporary Ireland*,[2] gives a better idea of the book's contents than did the original title *Le droit ecclésiastique contemporain d'Irlande*.

Ireland is unique in being the first country in modern times where a believing Catholic people, led by practising Catholics, established a democratic republic. Ninety-five per cent of the population of the Republic are Catholics and all political parties support the existing Constitution (that of 1937).

'One might think that the Church, in so Catholic a country, has a privileged legal status. Such is by no means the case. She has no official status. . . . From 1534 until modern times she

[2] Clonmore and Reynolds, Dublin, 1964.

has been either outlawed or tolerated, but never legally recognized.'[3]

Neither has the Church any financial claims on the State. In contrast to the general practice in European states (including several Communist ones), the Irish State does not endow religion or its ministers in any way. On the contrary, Church property is now taxed more widely than before independence.

The Irish State does not, however, distance itself formally from Christian belief—on the contrary. Since the State is democratic and all the political leaders are practising Christians (almost all of them Catholics), such an attitude would be impossible. The situation in the Irish Republic is, indeed, an example of how unimportant for the Church are State legal arrangements or State subsidies when almost the entire citizen body are in sympathy with the Church through their active Catholicism.

The preamble to the Constitution begins :

'In the Name of the Most Holy Trinity, from Whom is all authority and to Whom . . . all actions both of men and States must be referred'

and continues :

'Humbly acknowledging all our obligations to our Divine Lord, Jesus Christ, Who sustained our fathers through centuries of trial. . . .'

M. Blanchard cites this preamble as an instance of what he calls the 'interpenetration' of the civil and religious spheres.

Article 44 of the Constitution, dealing with Religion, states that the homage of public worship is due to Almighty God and continues :

'Art. 44 1, 2 : The State recognizes the special position of the Holy Catholic Apostolic and Roman Church as the guardian of the Faith professed by the great majority of the citizens. Art. 44 1, 3 : The State also recognizes the Church of Ireland, the Presbyterian Church in Ireland, the Methodist Church in

[3] Op. cit., p. 59.

Ireland, the Religious Society of Friends in Ireland, as well as the Jewish Congregation and the other religious denominations existing in Ireland at the date of the coming into operation of this Constitution.'

Further clauses guarantee freedom of conscience and declare that 'the State guarantees not to endow any religion' and not to discriminate on religious grounds. M. Blanchard comments (p. 68) on the reference to the Catholic Church :

'What significance is to be attributed to "recognition of the special position". . . ? No legal steps have been taken to clarify and amplify this text.'

Elsewhere (p. 70) M. Blanchard writes :

'The Church has no legal personality; parishes and bishoprics are not persons in civil law. Consequently . . . the Church itself cannot possess property or take legal proceedings; she must have recourse to the system of Trustees.'

And, on p. 69 :

'Thus there is no ministry for religion, or no religious subsidy departmental service, in the charge of the Prime Minister or other minister, to look after the relations with the Church authorities. There are no religious questions per se, public life being religious, since the nation is devoutly Christian.'

Not only does the State not subsidize the Church,

'it does not recognize her right to levy taxes to provide for the needs of the clergy or maintain religious buildings, as is done in Spain for instance. . . . The clergy receive no assistance or salary from the Irish State.'

The entire income of the Church is derived from the voluntary gifts of the people.

The civil and religious calendars are not in agreement : feasts like the Ascension and the Assumption are not public holidays in Ireland. The State censorship of books takes no guidance from the Roman Index; it does not concern itself with ideological or philosophical questions. There is no Concordat between Ireland

and the Holy See for the simple reason that none has been considered necessary. The civil power has no veto in the choice of bishops.

'The Church, separated from the State, does not interfere, at least directly, in the functioning of the latter. She takes no direct part in politics, at least in the sense that her clergy do not sit in Dáil Éireann (the national Parliament). In addition, she carefully adopts a neutral attitude towards the parties who, it is true, all appeal to Catholic doctrine. . . . The Church, though this seems paradoxical, appears less active in this field than she was before independence. . . . It was not unusual, at that time, to see a parish priest presiding at a political meeting' (Blanchard, pp. 71-2).

This does not mean, of course, that the bishops, either individually or collectively, do not occasionally state their views or give doctrinal rulings on political matters (medical aid legislation, IRA terrorism) when they believe that an important moral issue is involved.

Divorce is prohibited by the Constitution. The civil code of matrimonial law, which was taken over from the British régime, recognized only the marriages of Protestants and ignored Catholic marriages. At present there is no civil matrimonial code for Catholic, Jewish, or Quaker marriages. Since canon law is not recognized by the State, difficulties of the kind mentioned above occur from time to time when matrimonial cases are before the courts. M. Blanchard cites court cases to show that an evolution has been taking place in the courts since independence. Not only in matrimonial cases, but in civil actions by clergy against their superiors, more notice has been taken of canon law and certain general non-religious provisions of the Constitution have been interpreted so as to take *de facto* cognizance of the rights of Catholics acting in obedience to their Church; for instance prenuptial promises about the education of children have been accepted as legally binding. Nevertheless, the courts are liable to over-rule the express decisions of the Roman Rota. In 1955 a decree of nullity granted by the Rota was ignored by an Irish court, which refused to declare the marriage void. If such clashes are to be completely avoided, either civil law or canon law—or both—will have to be amended.

M. Blanchard points out that although the two powers, Church and State, coexist separately, in practice they collaborate in certain spheres. The outstanding example is education. In the case of primary education (up to fourteen years of age), the State pays the teachers and provides two-thirds of the building costs of a new school. It prescribes the curriculum, inspects its fulfilment, and sets examinations. The schools are, however, managed and the teachers appointed by the local parish priest. The same system applies to Protestant and Jewish schools, which are managed by their respective ministers of religion. Most Catholic secondary schools are run by religious Orders. The State pays a money grant for every secondary school pupil (of whatever denomination) on condition that the school observes certain rules.

Commenting on the Church-State relationship in general, M. Blanchard writes (p. 76) :

'The Church adjusts itself to the existing situation . . . although it is not, in theory, in accordance with the requirements of canon law. The Church . . . deems it better not to seek to obtain more. She has never protested against this régime.'

In his book *Studies in Political Morality* (published in 1962)[4] Dr Jeremiah Newman, Professor of Sociology at Maynooth College, disagrees with several aspects of Fr Courtney Murray's thesis on the Church-State relationship and describes the Constitution of Ireland as 'a model framework of Christian democracy'.

The proclamation which was issued at the start of the Irish revolution in 1916 undertook to 'cherish all children of the nation equally'. The reflection of this principle in the Constitution and its conscientious application to the civic rights of all citizens, irrespective of religion, has done much to establish good relations between the different denominations. The political issue between Irish and English (or between Irish and Anglo-Irish) had become, since the Reformation, largely an issue between a

---

[4] Scepter, Dublin.

Catholic people and a Protestant ruling class whose allegiance was to Britain. The State which was estabished after independence wisely refrained from any vindictiveness. The Protestants were left in possession of most of the old cathedrals and churches. The first President of the Republic was a Protestant, and Protestants have been elected mayors of the major cities. There has even been a tendency to favour Protestants more than their numbers would justify. For example, the national television service allots one out of every five religious programmes to Protestants, although their numbers would justify only one in twenty.

This more than tolerant attitude has been partly due to a desire to mark the difference in this respect between the Republic and Northern Ireland. The latter, which is still attached to Britain, has been governed for the past forty years by a Protestant political party which does not admit Catholics to membership. This Government has failed to implement social justice for the substantial Catholic minority in the spheres of local government, housing, and employment.

There can be no doubt that the Constitution of the Republic and its implementation have provided a valuable practical service to the cause of ecumenism. The Irish Constitution has often been quoted by American Catholics to allay the fears of those American Protestants who believe that a Catholic government must necessarily be intolerant and must necessarily make Catholicism the State religion. Irish Catholics and Protestants in the Republic are gradually changing their attitude towards each other. Leading Protestant personalities in the religious and secular spheres have frequently expressed appreciation of the way Protestants have been treated by the Irish State since independence. The situation of the Catholic people in Northern Ireland continues, however, to provide an obstacle to full Catholic confidence in Protestant goodwill.

In a recent address,[5] the Bishop of Cork and Ross, Dr Cornelius Lucey, said that the special difficulties facing the ecumenical movement in Ireland were twofold. One was that there was no organized body of non-Christians to confront, although

[5] Report from *Catholic Standard*, 22 May 1964.

atheism and materialism did exist in various forms. The other was historical.

> 'In Ireland, the Protestant is for the Catholic not only a Protestant, but is associated with the dark past of the Ascendancy and penal times. Our immediate contribution to the ecumenical movement should be to forget the past and see our Protestant neighbours not as descendants of landlords, planters, and the rest, but as Irishmen like ourselves, differing from us in religion, but not one hundred per cent or even fifty per cent different.'

The immediate problem of Christians, he said, is to reach a better understanding with each other, to live and let live together, reserving their opposition for those not of Christ at all. The means to such better relations are dialogues between the different Churches.

2

TIME OF DECISION[1]

Whenever Rome calls for radical renewal of the Church, the most vigorous immediate support comes from those parts of Christendom where the Church is in acute crisis and where theology is alive. It is therefore hardly surprising that when Pope John called for a Council that would lead to a radical aggiornamento most of the leading personalities of the Irish Church showed little interest.

Measured in terms of the number of religious vocations, of popular and voluntary participation in the Church's liturgy, reception of the sacraments, voluntary financial support of the Church, missionary enterprise, effective lay apostolate, relationship of Church to civil society in five-sixths of Ireland, and imaginative, practical expansion of the nineteenth-century formula of Catholicism, the Irish Church was flourishing. Measured by the standards of that late Tridentine Catholicism—of which modern Irish Catholicism was the most thorough-going, full-blooded and successful embodiment—this was more or less what the Church should be. What the modern Irish Church had received from its formative period in the nineteenth century had been conserved at home, while being made to bear fruit in fifty-three countries. The point had been reached where three out of every four priests ordained in Ireland were leaving to work in Britain or overseas—three hundred priests were being 'exported' annually. The Legion of Mary, which was founded by lay people in Dublin in 1921 and which had provided the backbone of the Church in China in face of Communist persecution, was publishing its bulletin in twenty-one languages and extending its apostolate in 1,300 dioceses at the rate of fifty new 'praesidia' a week.

[1] November 1964.

25

For over a century six major seminaries had been training priests almost exclusively for English-speaking countries abroad. One of them, St Patrick's College, Carlow, sent out priests as follows between 1920 and 1956 : U.S.A. 334, Britain 274, Australia 131, New Zealand 16, South Africa 10, France 2. Between the revolutionary years (1916-21) and the 1950s the missions to Africa and Asia were developed. 'Between 1933 and 1953 the number of missionaries sextupled', exclaimed the French magazine *Missi* in a broad survey of Irish Catholicism (April 1962). New Irish congregations of nuns, streamlined for modern missionary work (e.g. the Missionary Sisters of St Columban, the Missionary Sisters of the Holy Rosary, the Medical Missionaries of Mary) covered the English-speaking world with their foundations and established hospitals, missions, and schools throughout Africa and Asia, breaking down the canonical and other taboos which hindered women's mission work, attracting and producing women of extraordinary character : to name but two, 'Mama Kevina' of Uganda and Mother Mary Martin, foundress of the Medical Missionaries. When the Council opened, hundreds of lay professional people were in Africa as mission-helpers.

To put it another way : when the call for aggiornamento reached the Irish Church, those members of its élite and of its rank and file who had remained in Ireland were very busy. There were the heavy tasks of organizing the missionary work and of training the great numbers of novices and seminarians : 75 seminarians per 100,000 Catholics—as compared with the next highest figures, 36 per 100,000 for Canada and 33-26 for Australia, Spain, Britain, and U.S.A. (*Herder-Korrespondenz*, May 1955). Moreover, most of the secondary education of Irish Catholics is provided in schools run by priests, nuns, or brothers. Although the number of Catholic priests in the Republic and Northern Ireland had increased by 87% since 1871—despite a 23% fall in the Catholic population through emigration—the absolute ratio of priests to people was not extraordinarily high : 558 Catholics per priest in 1960. This figure includes non-diocesan priests, whose numbers had increased between 1871 and 1961 by 396%. In Holland the ratio of Catholics per priest was 494, in Britain 507, in France (which is said to be very short of priests) 751, and in

Italy 766, although 28 Italian dioceses had a ratio of less than 400 to 1.[2] In the Anglican Church of Ireland the ratio of church-members to ministers was 180 to 1.[3]

Besides, in order to interpret the Irish Catholic priest-people ratio correctly, one must take into account that almost the entire Catholic population are regular practicants. The demands made on the 58% of priests who are directly engaged in pastoral work are therefore unusually high.

'Our position is quite extraordinary,' writes Daphne D. C. Pochin Mould. 'We are a people who take the existence of God for granted and, I suppose, alone in the modern world, a nation that attends Sunday worship regularly as a taken-for-granted universal custom.'[4]

In an article in *Études* in May 1964 Fr John C. Kelly, S.J., tries to take a sober view of Irish religious practice. Remarking that some people would say that social pressures play a part in the large attendance at Sunday Mass and that there may be some truth in this, he goes on to say :

'On the other hand, in Dublin, and certainly in the country, people undergo real hardship, without complaining, to attend Sunday Mass. They are present Sunday after Sunday in circumstances which, in the opinion of even the strictest moral theologian, would excuse them from attendance. . . . There are some more facts that give one pause. The most important of these is the number of people in Dublin who attend morning Mass on weekdays before going to work. This is one of the phenomena of Dublin (population 650-700,000). From 6.30 in the morning until about 8.30 there are large congregations at Mass and many receive Holy Communion. This is certainly sincere. . . . On feasts of the Church and particularly at the Easter liturgy, in more than one Dublin Church as many as ten thousand hosts must be consecrated so that the huge numbers of people present may receive Holy Communion. It is im-

---

[2] Figures from Jeremiah Newman's 'The Priests of Ireland : A Socio-Religious Survey', *The Irish Ecclesiastical Record*, July 1962.
[3] Kevin Smyth, S.J., *The Furrow*, March 1958.
[4] *The Furrow*, February 1964.

possible to think that most of these people are not genuine and sincere. They are under no obligation. They act freely.'

Attendance at weekday Mass increased rather than diminished during the 1950s. Most urban churches have at least six Masses on Sunday morning. The scene outside a Dublin suburban church between two Sunday Masses, with police on special traffic duty, special Mass-buses arriving and departing, and perhaps two hundred cars parked or moving slowly through the crowded streets, is one which explains many things about Irish Catholicism —about its strength and its problems—to the sensitive observer. (There is a common misconception that Irish Catholicism, almost entirely urban in its foreign transplantations, is still closely connected with agriculture at home. In this regard, it should be taken into account that only 35% of the working population of the Republic are engaged in agriculture.)

However, amid all this activism and partly because of it, theology and philosophy slumbered. Theology was accepted as something finished and given, not as something in need of constant re-making through the personal confrontation of knowing Christians with the truth of Christ and his Church.

It was not, as the cliché would have it, that Irish priests were 'unintellectual' or 'anti-intellectual'. They included all types and some of them could be thus described. Many, on the other hand, have been outstanding scholars in various spheres of secular learning. For many decades past, all of them have received a thorough theological training. It was the attitude to theology of the 'intellectual' priests which was the real fault. Their concept of intellectual endeavour in the theological sphere was too narrowly rationalistic and too exclusively bound up with scholastic textbooks and commentaries. The intellectualism which they practised was typically late Tridentine—legalistic, positivistic, academic. Their arid, doctrinally correct sermons were often too abstract, too untouched by life—by the lives of the individual preachers to begin with. Due to this stagnation of theology, there were few voices in Ireland to say with authority that late Tridentine Catholicism, however 'successful' in its Irish embodiment, was not enough for Christian men and women, that it omitted too much of life. While this was being said by a growing number of theologians in the French- and German-speaking parts of the continent—while the present radical restatement of Christianity was being prepared by men deeply involved in the acute crisis of their own local churches—the leaders of the Irish Church seemed intent merely on holding the bastion of Irish faith and practice; most of the innovating personalities and tendencies were channelled (some might say forced) into missionary activism abroad.

During the period between 1920 and the Second World War the single far-reaching innovation in the strictly internal life of Irish Catholicism was, oddly enough, the work of laymen. The establishment of the Irish State and the framing and implementation of the Constitution of 1937 not only effected a radical change in the temporal circumstances of Irish Catholicism and opened new possibilities for its redemptive action. As the work of Catholics, assented to by a Catholic people, it ushered in a form of Church-State relations and of Catholic relationship to modern civil society which had no precedents. But there have been other changes in the life of the Irish Catholic people since 1920 which, in their cumulative effect, were pointing towards the necessity for a radical restatement of the Christian message: increasing access to secondary and higher education; widening experience in all fields; the weakening of Irish nationalism as a buttress to Catholic belief and practice; the consequent ideological vacuum and the impact of liberal materialism both on the people at home and, even more so, on the million Irish-born Catholics now living in Britain; increasing affluence; large-scale movement from the country to (Irish and English) cities. Due, however, to the stagnation of theology, the Irish Church failed to make an adequate creative response to these changes (cf. Nivard Kinsella, in *Rural Ireland*[5]). Thoughtless condemnation and thoughtless approval were poor substitutes.

In the years between the Second World War and the Council a movement towards the intensification of Catholic life in Ire-

[5] Published annually by Muintir na Tíre Publications, Tipperary.

land got under way. It was not a 'movement' really until the
Council came and gathered all its forces together. It was a series
of decisions and initiatives which were not inspired by any new
theological vision of Irish origin, but which implied a new concern for the quality of Irish Catholic life. Perhaps it was partly
due to the imposed isolation of the war years, when Ireland
remained neutral. During these years certain imaginative personalities of the Irish Church may have been forced to be interior,
to turn in on themselves.

In the fifteen years before the Council the two journals were
founded which were to act as literary focal points for the new
currents : *The Furrow*, edited from Maynooth by Dr J. G. Mc-
Garry, and *Doctrine and Life*, edited by Austin Flannery, O.P.,
in Dublin. New institutes and congresses were founded : an annual
Irish Liturgical Congress in the Benedictine Abbey of Glenstal;
the Dublin Institute of Catholic Sociology, sponsored by the
Archbishop of Dublin, Dr John Charles McQuaid; the Christus
Rex movement of priest sociologists (with its journal of the same
name edited by Dr Jeremiah Newman of Maynooth); the Social
Study Congress in Dublin. The Jesuits opened a college for trade
unionists. Irish publishers, with the Mercier Press of Cork in the
lead, translated many German and French theological works.
Old-established Catholic journals passed into the hands of new
editors and showed marked improvement. Biblical studies made
some progress despite episcopal restraints. Pre-marital courses for
engaged couples and young married people were established at
several centres. *Doctrine and Life* began the publication of a
special journal for nuns. Summer courses and study meetings of
all kinds multiplied. An excellent vernacular Ritual in Irish and
English was adopted. Some architects, priests, sculptors, and
painters began to collaborate fruitfully for the renewal of church
architecture and sacred art.

Far from producing complacency, this new 'movement' was
accompanied by growing dissatisfaction with the status quo and
by increasing concern about the future. From about 1957 onwards sharp public self-criticism began : by priests of themselves
and their fellow-clergy, by laymen of the clergy and of the Irish

Church structure as a whole. This criticism was encouraged by the Council and by the progressive propaganda which accompanied it. At present it is both widespread and intense. The well-known negative criticisms of Irish Catholicism by Irishmen and by foreigners have been faced up to and analysed by priests (cf., for example, Denis Meehan, *The Furrow*, April 1957 and August 1960; Kevin Smyth, S.J., *ibid.*, March 1958; Seosamh Ó Nualláin, *ibid.*, April 1958).

The contribution by Fr Smyth, a theologian and biblical scholar, was especially significant, since it was originally read as a paper to the Maynooth Union Summer School in 1957. Some of his introductory remarks offered a basis for the further critical discussion and could have helped to make it constructive—if they had been heeded :

'The healthy state of the [Irish] Church is so obvious that anything like an orgy of self-criticism would be unbalanced and pointless. Whatever may be called for in Latin America, in Italy, or France, there is no need here for a dirge to a decaying priesthood, an estranged and dechristianized people. However, we priests are perfectionists . . . we echo Mao Tse Tung in China recently : "Let a hundred flowers of criticism bloom, let schools of thought contend." There may be some defects in what Continental Catholic intellectuals call "le catholicisme du type irlandais". There may be certain manifestations of anticlericalism in our country which are depressing if not terrifying. There may be instances of a lack of soundness in the moral fibre and religious sense of the Catholics whom we produce. While listening for the discords, we must not be deaf to the great fundamental harmonies which have produced what is perhaps the most solid achievement of Catholic culture in the world, an achievement hard to parallel elsewhere, except in Catholic bodies which are precisely modelled on the *type irlandais*, namely the Church in England, America, and Australia.'

Other writers have gone beyond the well-worn lines of criticism to formulate personal critiques (cf. John C. Kelly, S.J., *Doctrine and Life*, October-November 1959; Desmond Fennell, *ibid.*, May

1962; John A. Dowling, *The Furrow*, March 1964). The debate eventually spread to the seminaries, the universities, the newspapers, and television. *Evening Press*, *The Irish Times*, and *Hibernia* made useful contributions.

Television discussions of Irish Catholicism by young lay people brought shocks, amazement, gratification, and displeasure into many homes. If the participants had been chosen because of their knowledge of Irish Catholicism and of Catholic life generally, these discussions would have been even more useful than they were—certainly more constructive. As it was—and as so frequently happens when Irish Catholics are discussing their country or their religion—intensity of feeling was often mistaken for knowledge and thought both by the participants and by many who heard them. A great deal of this widened public debate was bedevilled by ignorance and provincial-mindedness. Very little effort has been made by Irish Catholics to study their Catholicism systematically, to amass or to publish rationally ordered knowledge of it. Hence, the provincial assumption that it was the best thing in the world shifted easily—under the impact of fashion and unhampered by knowledge—to the even more provincial-minded conviction that it was the worst thing and that the proper norms of human and of Christian living were all to be found elsewhere.

The reaction away from the inherited Catholicism has been accompanied by a reaction away from nationalist ideology. This coincidence and the resulting ideological vacuum have confused the issue very much indeed. Unfortunately, Irish churchmen had failed to supply the practising, believing Catholics who govern and administer the country and who live in it as citizens with positive Christian inspiration for their temporal concerns and activities. The Prime Minister, Mr Seán Lemass, had to wait for Pope John's encyclicals to get effective Christian guidance for his Government's social policies.

Thus the reaction away from nationalism has been accompanied in many cases by an atavistic return to reliance on England for ideological inspiration—and this means a turning towards liberal materialism. Irish liberal materialists and anti-Catholics have had a heyday as soured Catholics gathered round them. Trinity College, the more or less Protestant university which has not quite outlived its colonialist tradition, has acted as a focal point for negativism. *The Irish Times*, a Protestant-owned newspaper and a sort of Irish version of the English *Guardian*, has played a provocative 'outsider's' role, publishing variations on the theme that 'you Irish [Catholics] are not as good as you think you are'. Part of the vogue is to look 'realistically' at Irish (read 'Irish Catholic') life. This is tacitly identified with looking at its seamy side and in the light of secular criteria, not of Christian supernaturalism. Some have discovered that 'liberal and enlightened opinion' is the norm which Christians should conform to. Amid such confusion students, journalists, and others can be heard lecturing clergy and people in these terms: 'Listen to Pope John and Karl Rahner, do what the Labour Government did in Britain (in the late 1940s) and approve of those things which *The Guardian* and the London *Observer* approve of.' In short, provincial-mindedness is having a fresh innings under new forms.

Amid the welter of self-assertion and of ideological manoeuvring many Catholics whose first concern is that their Church increase in Christian fruitfulness look expectantly and apprehensively towards their bishops. Clergy and laymen, they form a sort of a seething underground. They want to graft the best of the new Church life on to Irish Catholicism. Most of them now believe that this is not merely a desirable thing but the only way to save the Irish Church from a sudden, acute crisis.

This more urgent note was heard in the writings and public statements of Irish Catholics some time after the movement of self-criticism had got under way. The transition to this view of the future can be noticed in a lecture which Fr P. Corcoran, S.M., gave in 1958. Fr Corcoran said:

'The danger, I think, is that we have made vast progress with our secular education; we have not made anything like the same progress with our religious education in relation to new needs. . . . I am aware that we possess a vast capital of strong faith inherited from the ages of persecution . . . (but) we cannot afford

B

to live just on this capital, otherwise it will be eaten away imperceptibly.'

When, in *Doctrine and Life* of May 1962, Desmond Fennell published an essay entitled 'Will the Irish Stay Christian?', his question was still so unspeakable and impolite that the title was changed on the cover of the magazine to the innocuous 'Ireland and Christianity'. Yet such was the positive response to this article that a few months later, when a comment by James Scott on the same theme was announced on the cover, the dread question was printed fearlessly. Mr Fennell's thesis was that Ireland could follow the rest of Europe away from Christianity through the failure of its Christian leaders to 'know the times', through a failure of intellect and charity combined.

In March of this year (1964) John A. Dowling, speaking on behalf of what he called 'interested, fair-minded, and educated Catholics', wrote :

'We fear, from personal experience, observation, and report . . . that Irish Catholicism has a predictably limited future as the faith of the mass of our people.'

His essay was a meditative reflection on the present feelings of the committed Catholic intelligentsia about their bishops. The Irish bishops had gone to the Council and had said very little. It seemed they had been taken by surprise. They returned and said very little.

One of the factors that sounded alarm in Ireland during the 1950s was the news from the Irish Catholic 'frontier' in England. At home there was a trickle of defections from faith and practice, but the news from England was of large-scale defections of Irish-born Catholics. During the nineteenth and early twentieth centuries Irish Catholics went in large numbers to Britain. Because of the political differences, the prejudices against them, and their largely irremediable poverty, they lived for the most part in Irish Catholic 'ghettos'. In this way they held the faith, and the defections, such as they were, occurred among their descendants. With the falling away of the political tensions in recent decades and with the easy mobility of labour and avail-

ability of employment in Britain during the 1950s, the relationship of Irish immigrants to British society changed.

In June of this year Fr Owen R. Sweeney published in *The
Furrow* an investigation he had made into sources of dissatisfac-
tion with the Irish Church among Irish-born Catholics in Britain.
In his introduction he states:

> 'From close observation, priests on the Emigrant Mission are
> agreed that, granted reasonable opportunities and a little
> interest in them by the local clergy, about 80% to 85% of our
> emigrants in Britain are devout in the practice of the faith,
> another 10% to 15% might be careless, and between 5% and
> 10% might be considered to have abandoned the practice of
> the faith—though very few would choose to die without the
> sacraments. . . . Taking the Irish-born population of Britain
> today at a million, even 5% to 10% lapsed still means some-
> where between 50,000 and 100,000 lapsed Irish Catholics in
> Britain, and the 10% to 15% careless means a further 100
> to 150 thousand who are "in danger"—figures which give the
> Church no grounds for complacency.'

Such losses among Catholics moving from a largely rural environment (most of the emigrants are country people) into large
dechristianized cities have long been accepted as normal in many
parts of the continent. But they shocked the Irish Catholic conscience, since this is the first time in its history that the Irish
Church has suffered such losses among its faithful. However, it
was not only the present losses in Britain which gave cause for
serious concern; the entire record of Irish Catholicism trans-
planted to Britain was not very heartening. True, Archbishop
Heenan, when Bishop of Leeds, could write (in *The Month*,
March 1957):

> 'One of the chief reasons for the over-crowding of our Catholic
> churches is the advent of so many practising Catholics from
> across the water.'

It was also doubtless true that Irish Catholic immigration was the
principal reason why more than 40% of the babies born in

London were receiving Catholic baptism. Compared, however, with the fruits of Irish emigration to America, the fruits of a hundred and fifty years of migration to Britain were disappointing.

It is at least possible, then, that one way or another that part of *le catholicisme du type irlandais* which is to be found in Ireland is moving towards a turning-point. If this 'crisis' (in the neutral and original meaning of the word) should take the form of radical renewal, the Irish reformers would be dealing with a reality very different from that which faces the reformers, say, on the European Continent.

The mistake has often been made, both in Ireland and abroad and by admirers as well as critics, of regarding the *type irlandais* as something absolutely *sui generis*. This naïve view leaves out of account the close relationship of the Irish Church to Rome during the period (the pontificate of Pius IX) when modern Irish Catholicism acquired its definitive content and shape, and its continuing closeness to Rome right up until the eve of the Council. In no other part of Catholic Europe did the late Tridentine formula of the Roman Church achieve such preponderance among clergy and people. At the time when this Roman formula was being implanted—and partly as a result of the thoroughness of its application—the Irish were losing their native language in a definitive manner and, with it, most of the native Christian culture which still linked them with their past.

The rebuilding of Irish Catholicism was done in English. A religion formulated in continental cities and seminaries and spread from Irish cities and towns largely replaced the traditional peasant religion. Devotions to Irish saints and other forms of traditional piety almost disappeared. First, French and renascent English Catholic devotionalism, later, the ordinary, Rome-approved Catholic devotional life of the twentieth century took their place. Part of the critical writing of recent years has come from priests who recall the scriptural and liturgical devotion, the richly human piety, and the love of beauty in the early and medieval Irish Church (with its aristocratic and mandarin culture) and in the peasant Catholicism which followed it (cf., Donnchadh Ó

Floinn, *The Furrow*, December 1954; Diarmuid Ó Laoghaire, *ibid.*, January 1956).

The centuries of persecution and destruction had also played their part in loosening the hold of tradition and reducing the material survivals of the past. Due to the shortage of priests, the medieval parish system had been thinned out; the cathedral chapters had disintegrated—there were no cathedrals for them. With very few and unimportant exceptions, the 2,500-odd churches in which Catholics worship in Ireland today were built during the nineteenth and twentieth centuries. So were nearly all the religious houses. No ancient statues or carved wooden altars look down at the worshippers. Unfortunately, the modern Irish Church acquired almost its entire material embodiment during an age when architecture and allied arts were at a low ebb and when Christianity, in common with the most powerful secular ideologies, was anti-art. Italian bad taste filled the new Irish churches (cf. Ray Carroll, *The Furrow*, August 1964).

Together, then, the age of persecution and the cultural break in the nineteenth century resulted in this: that the new Irish Church was almost totally unencumbered by dead baggage or by mortgages from the past and was very poor, materially and culturally. There was not even an *ancien régime* in the background for reactionaries to hark back to or for progressives to use as a bogeyman. Modern Irish Catholicism had the freedom and strength which youth and poverty offer. Because it was rich in faith it was able to use them.

The most decisive factor in making this Catholicism seem 'un-European' to Continental Catholics was not its 'Irishness' but its centuries-old contact with English culture, which in the nineteenth century became an immersion. It was by adopting the English language, important elements of English political practice and of English civil and middle-class morality, that the Irish produced a Catholicism which was European in its roots and yet transcended Europe. This was the cultural situation which a century ago induced Cardinal Newman to say:

'I contemplate a people which has had a long night and will have an inevitable day. I am turning my eyes towards a hundred years to come and I divinely see the island I am gazing on become the road of passage between two hemispheres —the centre of the world.'

English culture was the Irish Catholic highway to the world outside Europe, and the first and second British empires the material and human basis of Irish Catholic expansion. Between 1830 and 1930 the legal Irish arrivals in the United States alone numbered four million. Without the English connexion, there would not be two thousand churches in five continents consecrated to St Patrick. English policies towards Ireland produced Irish nationalist ideology—a Protestant and secularist creation which the Catholics eventually used. Without the English provocation, late Tridentine Catholicism would not have found in the Irish Catholics a people whose religious enthusiasm was reinforced by the enthusiasm and vitality of an oppressed nation striking out for justice and freedom.

Although the nationalist ideology drew its original inspiration from the French and American revolutions and although the revolutionary movement in the decisive years had friendly relations with the Russian Bolsheviks, the immediate (provocative) model for Irish nationalism was English nationalism. It can even be said that the British, by providing an empire for the Irish to revolt from, put Ireland in the forefront of one of the decisive world movements of the twentieth century—anti-colonialism— and eased the way, humanly speaking, for the Irish missionaries in Africa and Asia. It was in the first year of the revolution, 1916, that a professor from Maynooth College and another priest founded the Maynooth Mission to China (which today has hundreds of priests in Asia), thereby giving the signal for the extension of missionary activity from the English-speaking countries to Asia and Africa.

Two further factors, which are bound up with the foregoing, must be noticed if the *catholicisme du type irlandais* is to be understood : first, the character of the Irish priest, his role in Irish life, and his relationship to the people; secondly, the proletarian and democratic character of modern Irish Catholicism in

its formative period and the consequent 'leftist' heritage of Irish
Catholicism today.

Dr Jeremiah Newman has given a pretty comprehensive
account of the first of these factors. Writing on 'the human
reasons for the wealth of priestly vocations in Ireland', he
attributes these partly to the effect produced in the consciousness
of the people by

'the respected place which the clergy, secular and regular,
have occupied in Irish life for well over a century. . . . For
centuries religion and patriotism went hand in hand in Ireland;
the priests were leaders of the people in many national movements; they helped their country rise from political and social
depression. The memory of this is still ripe in Irish minds. . . .
And by reason of the absence of any subsidy from the State,
the clergy are in no danger of being regarded as public officials.

'Hand in hand with this goes an appreciation of the Irish
priest as a man of culture. For decades he has been in the forefront of cultural development—intellectual, athletic, and the
like. . . . Yet though well equipped intellectually, the Irish
priest and more especially the diocesan priest is not given to
cultural snobbism. Indeed if anything he tends to conceal his
learning and to concentrate on taking part in the everyday
life of the people. . . . He mixes well and engages in all lawful
activities. In short, while he is known by the people to be a
well-educated as well as a spiritual man, he tends to act and to
be prized by them, as a manly friend and fellow-citizen rather
than as a scholar.

'There are no minor seminaries in Ireland of the kind that
are found in most Continental dioceses. It is not our custom in
Ireland to set apart students for the priesthood at an early
age, put them into soutanes and bring them up in the protected
atmosphere of exclusively clerical surroundings.'[6]

Dr Newman also stresses the important role of sport and athletics
in the training of priests in Ireland.

[6] Extracts from paper by Dr Newman in *Die Europäische Priesterfrage*,
Internationales katholisches Institut für kirchliche Sozialforschung, Vienna,
1959.

Un catholicisme prolétaire is the heading of one of the sections in the *Missi* account of Irish Catholicism which we mentioned at the start. The proletarian origins of modern Irish Catholicism can be sufficiently illustrated by the fact that at the end of the eighteenth century Catholics owned eight per cent of the Irish land and their Church no land at all. Daniel O'Connell's organization of the rural millions into a political force provided a model which many Irish Catholics later followed in their organization of political parties and labour movements abroad. Throughout the nineteenth century and during the revolutionary years, the Irish Catholics stood on the European 'left', and this tradition, reinforced by the anticolonial revolution, has been inherited by the present Irish State.

If the Republic were not governed by practising Catholics who profess allegiance to the social encyclicals of Pope John and if the terms 'right' and 'left' were taken seriously in Irish politics (which they are not), then the present Irish State-society would be described as 'leftist'. The circumstances of its origin, the decisive role of public ownership in the economy (much greater than in Sweden, say, after thirty years of 'Socialist' government), the Church-State relationship, the commitment to social redistribution of income and control of private business, the virtual abolition of capital punishment, the relative classlessness of society, Irish loyalty to UNO, and Irish policies in the United Nations Assembly on Communist China, nuclear disarmament, and the Afro-Asian nations, Ireland's non-membership of NATO—all these factors would qualify the Irish State-society as 'left', and consideration of this fact helps to characterize the human circumstances in which Irish Catholicism is developing.

None of the Irish political parties includes the word 'Christian' in its title and Irish Catholics do not relish this aspect of Catholic political organization on the Continent. The only political party in Ireland with a denominational commitment is the Unionist Party in Northern Ireland, which is specifically a Protestant party. But its record during forty years of government does not commend it as a model to Irish Catholics. (To be exact, a small 'Christian Democratic Party' exists, but none of its members has been elected to Parliament.) Neither are there officially 'Catholic' trade unions or universities. Government policy has frequently been described as 'pragmatic' and 'undoctrinaire'. (American readers will note the parallel with President Kennedy's 'Irish Mafia'.) The fact that 95% of the population and most of the politicians are Catholics has, of course, had some influence on Government policies; but it has, on the whole, been a preventive rather than a positive influence.

To sum up : modern Irish Catholicism is not *sui generis*. Since it is a part of the Catholic Church, this would be a contradiction in terms. Late Tridentine Catholicism was fused in Ireland with cultural elements which were drawn mainly from English Protestant and secular culture, but which were embodied by a non-English people whose modern history had been very different from that of the other European Catholic peoples. (The fact that the famous 'low Irish marriage rate' and the lateness of marriage in Ireland—features which are now improving—were lower and later among Protestants than among Catholics is a detail which shows how misleading it can be to view nineteenth-century Irish Catholic history in isolation from its Protestant environment.) The closest European parallels with modern Irish Catholic history in its social and political aspects are to be found in German and Dutch Catholic history—especially the latter—in the eighty years or so before the First World War.

If the renewal proposed by the Council and by the reforming element in the Church is to become effective in Ireland, this should mean a new theology resulting in a new kind of priest and a new kerygma. Elements of the new kerygma would be liturgical and catechetical renewal, ecumenical initiatives, and a new evaluation of the layman's role. What are the chances?

To the extent that the renewal consists of external activities, forms, new words and phrases, assent to certain attitudes, the signs are that it will pass into Irish Catholicism without much ado. To a considerable extent, it has already done so. The new theological language has become normal in the better journals. *The Furrow* and *Doctrine and Life* have been so active in things ecumenical that the names of non-Catholic clergymen in their tables of contents no longer cause any surprise. There have been a few theological study meetings of Catholic and non-Catholic clergymen. Disinterest and reserve are still widespread, but the only real opposition comes from a section of Belfast Presbyterianism.

The bishops met in June 1964 and took decisions about the use of the vernaculars in the liturgy. These decisions were sent to Rome for approval without their contents being published. During the thirteen years of its existence the Irish Liturgical Congress has spread liturgical education among a considerable number of priests. It is difficult to gauge the attitude of the people and of the priests in general towards liturgical change. To judge by the laity's responses to minor innovations during the past decade, they are willing to adapt themselves to anything. There is a deep trust of the Church and, among the more educated, an experimental, expectant frame of mind. In secular affairs an experimental, innovating atmosphere is abroad. The Republic is experiencing an industrial boom, and the population is at last increasing. The people feel that their country and their society have still to be made—so that open-mindedness in regard to religious forms does not require much effort. The shyness—even secretiveness—of Irish Catholics about their religious life may put obstacles in the way of some liturgical innovations. The many very large churches and the sheer physical problems of handling and shifting the Sunday crowds within a limited time may also present difficulties. In a lecture given in Dublin, Fr M. A. Aussibal, O.P., of Lyons mentioned 'lack of religious practice' as one of the factors which has hastened the liturgical revival in France since the war (*Catholic Standard*, 4 September 1964).

Whatever the hazards of liturgical innovation in Ireland, empty formalism and self-admiring aestheticism are not among them. As things stand, the attachment to the liturgy is too deep and too massive for either of these distortions to occur. In an interview given to Radio Eireann in Rome during the second session of the Council, Fr Hans Küng, the Swiss theologian, said :

'I know that in Ireland approximately 90% of the Catholics go to Mass on Sunday. I think in this situation it is easier to make the renewal of the liturgy and to make it as soon as possible, so as not to lose the people we have lost on the Continent many decades ago. I think precisely Ireland could be the example to other countries how this renewal . . . of the liturgy could be done.'

Fr Johannes Hofinger, the expert on modern catechetics, broke new ground when, in the course of his ninth world tour in 1964, he gave courses in Ireland, Britain, and Africa. He attracted his biggest audiences to date when he visited Ireland in July. Two complete courses at Belfast and Waterford, plus a special three-day session for priests in Dublin, gave more than three thousand Irish catechists an opportunity of hearing him.

Both Belfast and Waterford were compelled to refuse hundreds of applications due to lack of space, while the former had to have recourse to a closed-circuit television service to accommodate its 1,300 participants. The composition of the combined audiences at the full courses was: 1,100 nuns, 1,000 lay teachers, 300 priests and brothers. In Northern Ireland two bishops paid the tuition fees for their teachers, while in the Republic the Department of Education recognized the course for the purpose of extra personal vacation for primary teachers. In addition to these courses, Archbishop Conway, Primate of All-Ireland, invited Fr Hofinger to address his priests on liturgy and catechetics. In all, Fr Hofinger delivered eighty hour-long conferences in twenty days. It was by far the biggest catechetical event ever held in Ireland.

What effect will these courses have on Irish catechetics? What surprised many was that the teachers were so interested. With very little publicity both centres were booked out well ahead of time, while many teachers drove more than a hundred miles a day to attend them. The simple explanation is that Irish catechists were better prepared than many realized.

Much quiet work had been going on behind the scenes. For example, many of the orders of nuns and brothers had been sending their members to study at such centres as Lumen Vitae, Jesus Magister and Regina Mundi. A few bishops had also sent priests abroad to study catechetics. These and other contacts with the movement had prepared the way, so that, while Fr Hofinger's ideas were a stimulant to all, they were not entirely new to a considerable number in his audiences. Over the past ten years or so the principles of the catechetical renewal have been disseminated mainly through summer courses which have now become a regular feature at all the bigger centres.

Although it cannot be claimed that the catechetical renewal has gained anything like general acceptance throughout the country, it can be said that already, inspired by the present renewal, some very good teaching of religion is being done in primary schools. So far, however, the present renewal has not influenced post-primary and pulpit catechesis to anything like the same extent that it has primary education; but a very significant step to remedy this has now been taken with the establishment, at the request of Archbishop McQuaid, of a lectureship in Catechetics at University College, Dublin, to train lay secondary and vocational teachers. (However, the news that the Douay version of the Bible has been prescribed for this course is, to say the least, not encouraging.)

Activating the laity is not a real problem in the Irish Church. Measured by the standards of lay apostolate and of secular Catholic achievement elsewhere, Irish lay Catholics have been very active indeed during recent decades. Specifically through secular activities they have opened new possibilities for the redemptive action of their Church. This has not prevented the 'question of the laity' from being discussed—and with the confusion which is often attendant on discussion of this theme. Those lay people who like most to talk about it often suffer from a clerical obsession—like the young man in a television discussion who criticized the parish clergy for not setting up lay Bible-reading groups! A desire to do something in the sacristy often becomes evident.

On the other hand, while the Legion of Mary has been a major contribution to the contemporary lay apostolate throughout the world, its impingement on Irish society has been marginal rather than central. Apart from limited progress by Opus Dei, no other form of organized lay apostolate has really taken root : large sectors of society are averse to the lay apostolate, regarding a man's religion as a very private matter and the task of spreading or deepening Christianity as the proper business of priests. A great deal of work remains to be done by theologians in making lay people conscious of the Christian value of their secular activities and in providing them with positive Christian inspiration for the specifically lay content of their lives. The indifference of the clergy to the Christian value of civil life and achievement often seems like ingratitude and lack of charity.

Hitherto there has been no crisis of obedience in the Irish Church. The directives which issue from Rome are implemented by bishops, priests and laity. This makes the personal attitudes of the bishops to Conciliar reforms of secondary importance. There has been much speculation about the bishops' attitude; hitherto episcopal procedure has been characterized by silence, obedience, and occasional enthusiastic support by individuals. Those who look to the bishops for innovating enthusiasm are often doing so merely on the analogy of the situation in those parts of the Continent where some brilliant bishops have pioneered the reforms. They forget that this has not been the way in which many important changes have come about in modern Irish Catholicism. Rather have the bishops often followed—resisting, restraining, guiding, governing—where the Christian people, laity and clergy, led.

It would certainly be unwise to assume that, because the call for radical renewal was not greeted in Ireland with wild enthusiasm, Irish interest in the new self-statement of Catholicism could never be more than moderate. The last major turning-point in the life of the Irish Catholic people occurred in the years 1916-19. When the armed revolution was started by a handful of visionaries, most of the Catholic people regarded them as madmen or criminals. Yet three years later the same people gave proof that those visionaries had divined their deepest desires correctly. In the British general elections of 1918 they abandoned the moderates whom they had supported previously and threw their support overwhelmingly behind the revolutionary party.

It is impossible to say towards what decisions Irish Catholicism is now moving, since, if faith holds and if things run true to form, these decisions at their most decisive will come from the people as a whole and from their theologians. If it is true that the most vigorous immediate support for radical renewal comes from those parts of Christendom where there is acute crisis and where theology is alive, it is also true that the most powerful ultimate support comes from those parts of the Church where the faith is strongest—and where theology rises to the occasion.

This is the second big imponderable : whether Irish theologians will rise to the occasion. This is the sphere in which the most difficult and the most fundamental contribution of a purely human kind needs to be made. It is the sphere in which mere profession of enthusiasm is least effective in producing a semblance of achievement. So far the new theological thinking which is being done in Rome and elsewhere has had a slight vivifying effect on Irish theologians. But the decisive break-through will come only when Irish theologians decide to imitate not the language merely, but the intellectual procedure of the best Continental theologians. This will mean restating Christian truth in terms derived simultaneously from close inspection of human life as it is presented in Ireland and from direct study of the ideal reality of the Church as presented by Revelation.

In this respect, almost everything remains to be done. Until it is done Irish Catholicism will be without its own new language —of word, image, and gesture—and the Irish Church will not be contributing all it could contribute to the universal renewal. Irish Catholicism needs vision—at first hand.

One consideration which argues against the fear that the Church in Ireland is heading for disaster is the enthusiasm—the absence of 'weariness'—among the pastoral clergy. High ambition, however naive sometimes, is met with everywhere. The Primate of All Ireland, Archbishop Conway, stated some months ago (in an interview given to *The Word* and quoted in *The Catholic Standard*, 26 June 1964) that Irish Catholics, because of their later, more gradual approach 'to the newer forms of modern civilization' had an 'opportunity to christianize this oncoming civilization to the core'. Such ambition does not seem inordinate to many Irish Catholics. If the faith holds firm and if the requisite theological leadership and episcopal collaboration are added to the high ambitions, the time may not be far distant when—in Ireland at least—a new Irish Catholicism will relegate *le catholicisme du type irlandais* to history.

In the course of the interview referred to above, Fr Hans Küng said :

'I saw in America and England how important is the position of the Irish in the Catholic world. I saw the great heart of the American and British hierarchy was Irish. . . . A great deal depends on Ireland how the renewal of all Christians is put into practice in a large part of the world. On the Continent people often think that the Catholic Church in Ireland is very "conservative", but I know that the Catholic Church in Ireland has a very, very great tradition and I know . . . that it is a living thing in the faith and practice of the people. At one time it was so on the Continent . . . I think we have done very many good things too late. You can do a lot of things we are doing now too late early enough. . . . Then with the radiation from Ireland of Irish population throughout the world, this will be of greatest importance for renewal of the Catholic Church in the world.'

3

IRISH CATHOLICS AND ENGLISH CATHOLICS[1]

While inter-denominational relations have improved considerably in every part of the British Isles except Northern Ireland, little progress has been made towards greater unity within English Catholicism or within the Catholicism of the British Isles as a whole. The main line of division is between 'pure English' Catholics and their adherents, on the one hand, and on the other the Hiberno-English and Irish Catholics. The historical roots of these divisions are deep and intricate.

The overall picture of progress in inter-denominational relations is not paralleled by any obvious signs of better relations among the different groups of Catholics who make up Catholicism in the British Isles. Fr Charles McGowan, writing to us from England last month, said :

> 'What I think we need today—more or less in the words of Pope John—is an attitude that is ecumenical not only to those outside the Church but also to those inside.'

The well-worn phrases 'French-speaking Catholicism' to indicate Catholics in France and Belgium, 'German-speaking Catholicism' to indicate the Catholicism of Germany, Austria and part of Switzerland, point a contrast with the situation in the British Isles. Most of the forward movement of the Church in Europe in recent decades has indeed come from those two areas of the Continent, where Catholics speaking the same language worked in essential unity, although divided by state boundaries.

The major barrier impeding Catholic unity in the English-speaking countries of Europe is a mixture of social, educational,

[1] April 1965.

political, and quasi-racial antagonisms with deep roots in history. It runs, on the one hand, through English Catholicism, dividing a smaller 'Pure English' part (which has its own divisions) from what Bernard Bergonzi, in his *Encounter* article last January, called the 'Hiberno-English mass'. But it also stands between the Pure English Catholics and Irish Catholicism proper—at least on the Pure English side.

In *Catholicisme anglais*[2] one of the contributing authors, Fr John Fitzsimons, refers to 'the fundamental contrast between the Catholic working class, almost entirely of Irish origin and voting Labour, and the minority, mostly English, who control the press and the organs of propaganda and are Conservative'. It is this minority who have hitherto largely shaped the public image of 'English Catholicism'. On the whole they have affected to ignore the 'Hiberno-English mass' and thus, in effect, working-class Catholicism in England. In the same book Fr Eugene Langdale says of the historians of English Catholicism :

'For them, the history of Catholicism in the nineteenth century seems to be summed up by the struggle alongside O'Connell for Catholic Emancipation, the Oxford Movement, the Count of Shrewsbury's foundations and Pugin's architecture, Newman's intellectual brilliance, and the great dynasty of Archbishops of Westminster, which began so majestically with Wiseman and Manning.'

Even the history of English Catholicism published in 1951 to mark the centenary of the re-establishment of the hierarchy 'does not', writes Fr Langdale, 'contain a single chapter on the influence of the Church among the working class'.

At the same time, and with a certain logic, this image-forming minority—with a few notable exceptions in the past such as Cardinal Newman and Chesterton—have made a point of sharing the attitudes of English chauvinists and anti-Catholic liberals towards 'the Irish' and towards 'Irish Catholicism' in particular. How unrepresentative these attitudes are of the feelings and con-

[2] Editions du Cerf, Paris, 1958.

victions of some English Catholics were exemplified in letters written to *The Tablet* after the publication of an article on 'Irish Catholicism' (25 July 1964). Presented as 'an Irish American's impressions' and generally hostile along well-worn lines, it was the only comprehensive account of the Catholic situation in Ireland offered by *The Tablet* during 1964. The reaction of several English correspondents showed that they saw the article as being primarily not a description but an attack, and that they sensed this attack to be an indirect advocacy of English liberal as opposed to Catholic values.

One correspondent (22 August 1964) wrote that the article consisted :

'of the usual litany of complaints launched regularly in the correspondence columns of the English Catholic press. . . . One expects the bright boys of *The Guardian* or *The New Statesman* to be shocked by the Church in Ireland. To them a Church with real power is a shocking thing. Their attitude over Malta is identical. But power abhors a vacuum, and if the power of the Church were removed, it would be replaced immediately by another power quite certainly worse. I am no apologist for Dr McQuaid (Archbishop of Dublin), but if I were compelled to chose between being ruled by him or by the faceless men of freemasonry and finance who control so much of our lives here, I would take a chance on the Archbishop of Dublin. As for the complaints about puritanism and censorship, these are the usual stock-in-trade of the liberal. When I look at the depraved faces of the hooligan gangs that infest our cities, I feel that one can pay too high a price for the freedom of the anti-clerical.'

Another correspondent, a priest, wrote (1 August 1964):

'I personally feel that the recent spate of criticisms of the Irish Catholic in the English Catholic press is unkind and unfair. It achieves nothing except to make the Irish Catholic feel unwanted and suspect. . . . Far more is achieved by a spoonful of honey than by a barrel of vinegar. . . . Too often the "poet critics", the "liberal minority", the "writers under constant siege" over-state their case and protest against the ills of the Church by their absence from its life-blood, the doers of the Word.'

A third correspondent (5 September 1964) joined with the first-mentioned in 'praying' that 'Irish Catholics will never enjoy the kind of "freedom" we have here—the freedom to be bullied, assaulted, deceived, corrupted, and robbed not only of our material possessions but of our faith in our fellowmen'.

That the passionate situation here revealed springs out of a real difficulty—or set of difficulties—is beyond dispute. In English history, but not in Irish or Scottish history, the reformed religion came to be identified unequivocally with the most authentic patriotism; Catholics became automatically suspect as probable sympathizers with the enemies of the realm. The political antagonism between the Catholic Irish and England in the nine-teenth century coincided with the first mass immigration of poor Irish Catholics and with that 'second spring' of native English Catholicism which derived its personnel and its brilliance from Oxford, High Anglican, and more or less upper-class circles. (Bernard Bergonzi's article in *Encounter* describes in some detail the various currents within Pure English Catholicism.)

In many parts of England, becoming a Catholic was des-cribed as 'going over to the Irish'. Irish Catholic culture and the Irish forms of piety—even the Irish Anglicans had gone very Low Church—were anything but attractive for Catholics whose cultural background was English and Anglican, their liturgical ideals High Anglican and Continental.

Aristocratic disdain and pseudo-aristocratic pretensions became mainstream characteristics of Pure English Catholicism. The zealous desire to prove political loyalty was strengthened by the compulsive urge to prove and assert one's cultural Englishness, even at the expense of one's Catholicity. This cultural compul-sion has been transferred to many English Catholics of Irish ancestry who have risen socially, thereby inducing in them a great deal of anguish which has little to do with the Catholic faith. (Cultural and political chauvinism among English Catho-

lics was a sort of parallel to the simultaneous efforts of many Irish
Catholics to become True Gaels first, Catholics second.)

The Irish Catholics of the first big migration—many indeed
of their Hiberno-English descendants as well—continued to sing
their hymn to St Patrick, 'dear saint of our isle', to recall past
wrongs done to Ireland, and to cherish Irish culture. Many of
them were openly hostile to England; not, however, to English
Catholics or English Catholicism, which they hardly ever encountered. The second big wave of immigration during recent
decades has added almost a million Irish citizens to the many-
layered Catholic Church in England. However, the improved
political relations of recent years between Ireland and England
have helped to remove the political element from inner-Catholic
tensions in England.

The hostility of many Pure English Catholics has not evoked
any parallel antagonism on the Irish side. The Irish Catholic
press carries on no feud against English Catholicism. One good
reason is that English Catholicism does not loom so large in the
Irish Catholic consciousness and field of vision as Irish Catholicism does in the consciousness and pre-occupations of native
English Catholics; England was only one of the directions in
which nineteenth-century Irish Catholicism expanded, and the
Irish Church is today involved directly in world-wide commitments. Only occasionally in conversation will Irish Catholics, in
England or Ireland, who have come up against Pure English
Catholicism, complain of 'coldness' or 'lack or charity'.

Two recent minor news items from the Catholic press reflect
the underlying complications and tensions. The English *Catholic
Herald* for 21 August reported the visit of a priest and of a band
of young musicians and dancers from a London parish to Rome
and Castelgandolfo. The children 'played a selection of Irish
tunes for Pope Paul' and 'gave a display of Irish dancing in St
Peter's Square'. When the same newspaper, which is read in
Ireland as well as Britain, was reporting Mr Pat Keegan's inter-
vention in the Vatican Council—'English lay apostle', 'first layman to address the Vatican Council'—the detailed account of
Mr Keegan's life portrayed him entirely as an English working

man and as the son of an Englishman. Three weeks later the readers of the Irish *Catholic Standard* in Ireland and Britain saw this headline : 'Patrick Keegan to be Mayo-Man of the Year?' The nominations for the award of this title by the Mayomen's association, said the *Standard*, included the name of Pat Keegan 'a native of Aughamore' (Ireland). The *Standard* seems to have been inaccurate—apparently Mr Keegan's parents were Mayo-born and he spent part of his childhood in Mayo, these facts being sufficient to qualify him for the award in question, which he eventually received; but the two radically different presentations illustrate the divisive tug-of-war going on beneath the surface. In deciding which English priests or laymen of Irish parentage should be dubbed 'Englishmen', English Catholics tend to be selective.

The incidents are not always trivial. When Cardinal Heenan spoke on religious freedom at the third session of the Vatican Council, some of the seventy bishops for whom he spoke were Irish. His praise of English religious liberty coupled with his failure to mention the only example of religious liberty in the English-speaking world for which Catholic statesmen are responsible caused understandable resentment in Ireland.

The entrenched positions remain, but the fronts are loosening, partly due to the break-up of the Hiberno-English proletariat. The liturgical reform, although it has called forth another division within English Catholicism between a 'Latinist' minority and the majority of worshippers, will help too by removing the former sharp contrasts between the 'Irish' and 'English' approaches to liturgy.

Translated into traditional English terms, the central tension in English Catholicism was a sort of parallel to the old, largely social and cultural antagonism between the High Anglican and the working-class Nonconformist. A hint of this shows through in an article by Auberon Waugh in the Chicago magazine *The Critic* (August-September 1964). Mr Waugh voices 'the unworthy suspicion that the Catholic clergy are using the ecumenical movement to make themselves more acceptable in English society'.

'For most laymen', he writes, 'the extent to which the Catholic clergymen are acceptable in Protestant circles is not a matter of great moment. Far more important is the way in which all this politeness is undermining the Church'.

After describing the Anglican Church as 'a happy church . . . its doctrine too vague to be controversial', he says :

'By contrast the Catholic Church was under-privileged, poor, and thriving. Its priests were from humbler stock. . . . Yet nobody doubted that the meaningful voice of Christianity in England was to be heard from Father Murphy's pulpit as he shouted about the danger of hell for reading Sunday newspapers, rather than from those fluting voices on the Bishops' Bench of the House of Lords, discoursing on the problems of leisure or the housing situation.'

There can be no doubt that the inner-Catholic fronts, the compulsive Englishness, the desire of some to please the powers that be at all costs, and the whole complex set of inner refusals to accept English Catholicism in its entirety, have made the impact of four and a half million Catholic Christians on English life so negligible as scarcely to be noticeable. A freely accepted sense of Catholic community is the prerequisite for a real contribution to the general English community. In the essay from *Catholicisme anglais* already quoted, Fr Fitzsimons remarks :

'The Catholics support each other on thorny issues such as the defence of their schools and their rights of the family, but in other domains their influence will remain weak for so long as they are not more united among themselves.'

The specific contribution of modern English Catholicism to English life has still to come. When it does come, it will inevitably be different from mere traditional Englishness and from any form of Englishness regarded as standard today.

The only groups who think in terms of a 'Catholicism of the British Isles' are, on the one hand, the Irish clergy and religious and the Legion of Mary—who contribute to pastoral work and to the apostolate in Britain—and, on the other hand, those Irish and English businessmen who sell specifically to the Catholic market. The general public consciousness of Catholicism in each country is insulated *vis-à-vis* the other. Neither in Ireland nor in Britain have the Catholic intellectuals so far managed to emulate the supranationalist concern and vision of Socialists of fifty years ago, such as James Connolly and Keir Hardie, for whom the British Isles constituted a common field of action.

Modern English-speaking Catholicism is only a century and a half old. Borne largely by a proletarian people and their priests, it intruded itself into a great culture which had turned its back on Roman Christianity. Only in Ireland did it have substantial roots in the past, and that past was not English-speaking. When these facts are taken into account the Catholic disunities in the English-speaking part of Europe can be seen in their true perspective as growing pains. In any organism, but especially in the Christian Church, the disadvantages of immaturity are more than balanced by its possibilities.

4

PROTESTANTS AND CATHOLICS

In the Irish Republic[1]

Two interesting contributions to the study of the Protestant minority in the Republic of Ireland have lately appeared. The first is an interview with the Anglican Archbishop of Dublin, Dr G. O. Simms, in the December 1964 issue of *The Word*, a monthly published by the Divine Word Missionaries in Ireland. The article broke new ground because it was the first time that the Archbishop had been interviewed by a Catholic journal.

The second, and more important, contribution is a notable series of five articles in *The Irish Times* for 22-26 March 1965, by an English journalist resident in Ireland, Michael Viney. Entitling his articles 'The Five Per Cent'—in token of the fact that the various Protestant denominations together make up only five per cent of the population of the Republic—Mr Viney offers a rounded picture of the Protestant community.

Both contributions contain tributes to the fair treatment of Protestants by the Catholic majority. Archbishop Simms, when asked 'Do you feel that Protestants are being fairly treated as a religious minority?' replied: 'Yes, I do think so. . . . We have a feeling that there is fair play for us.' Michael Viney reports that he asked a group of some thirty young Protestants, from all parts of the country, if they felt there was any discrimination known to them which might influence their choice of a career. No one could think of any.

The Protestant minority is heavily over-represented in the wealthier sections of the community. In Mr Viney's words, '65 in

[1] July 1965.

every thousand working Protestant men are directors, managers, and company secretaries; a further 83 will be in professional and technical jobs. In every thousand Catholic working men, only 9 will have reached executive posts and a further 43 will have professional and technical occupations.' In the countryside too, about a fifth of the farmers occupying the largest category of farms (those over two hundred acres) are Protestants.

Yet the impression left, particularly by Mr Viney's articles, is of a far from trouble-free community. The Protestant minority has a lower birth-rate than the Catholics, and has been declining in numbers. Especially in the south and west of the country, the Protestant denominations have to maintain, most uneconomically, clergymen who minister to tiny congregations scattered over immense areas. As the Anglican *Church of Ireland Gazette* put it, in an approving comment on Mr Viney's articles, the picture they give is of 'a Church that is happy enough to preserve as much as possible of its status quo'.

This attachment to a precarious status quo, based on the halcyon days of the Protestant Ascendancy, was dealt with at some length by two Church of Ireland clergymen, Canon John Barry and Rev Malcolm Graham, in a joint letter to *The Irish Times*. Referring to the fact that the two medieval cathedrals in Dublin are still in Protestant hands (the Catholics of Dublin having only a 'pro-cathedral'), the two clergymen wrote:

'We continue to maintain a full round of cathedral staff and services in two centres in Dublin, literally within sight of each other, when honestly speaking we have neither the people nor the money to do more than justify one. This is a situation that can only be explained by saying either that we have not yet fought a way through the mental confusion into which we were thrown at the downfall of the old Ascendancy, or that in some sub-Christian way we think that we must, at whatever cost, cling to things as they once were, since otherwise we would lose face. . . . There is an attractive mixture of self-interest and benevolence in the thought that we could do ourselves a good turn by loaning a Cathedral for, say, a hundred years to the Presbyterians or Roman Catholics—or any other Christian body who would revere its sacred purpose.'

Dealing with the general over-supply of Protestant churches in the Republic, the two clergymen went on to say :

'In number and size, our stock of parish churches is so far in excess of our capacity for keeping them in order that there is hardly a clergyman in a rural area who does not find himself with a major problem of repair on his hands. For many of them, institution to a cure of souls could be described more aptly as life-long committal to a campaign of money-raising to keep three of our buildings from disintegrating into the ground. In a word, a major defect in the Church of Ireland today is that spiritual life is in danger of being smothered under the weight of a vast accumulation of rubble and old mortar.'

Another area of difficulty is education. Primary and secondary education in Ireland are strictly denominational, and Protestant schools are entitled to the same support from the State as Catholic ones. The Department of Education, Mr Viney was told, 'has always treated us with scrupulous fairness', and has indeed subsidized transport schemes to bring scattered Protestant children in rural areas to schools of their own faith.

But there are problems in maintaining a network of separate schools for so small a minority. Protestant primary schools are mostly very small, with only one teacher to cater for all ages from six to fourteen. Protestant secondary schools receive the same subsidies as Catholic ones, but they find that the money does not go so far. Whereas Protestant teachers, being mostly married men, need all their salaries, Catholic teachers, being often members of religious orders, can plough part of the money back into their schools.

One possible ground for dissatisfaction on the part of the minority is the imposition of Catholic norms in matrimonial matters. In Ireland there is no provision for divorce, and the sale of contraceptives is banned. Archbishop Simms appears not to think this a serious grievance. When asked 'Do you think that many Protestants in the twenty-six counties would be in favour of divorce and birth control?' he replied : 'I don't think they would.' When, in fact, Irish Protestants (or Catholics) do wish to get divorced, they usually go to Britain. However, some of Mr Viney's informants resented the imposition on Protestants of legislation embodying (as they see it) Catholic beliefs. 'It's none of my business', said a Methodist student, 'if the Catholics forbid their people contraceptives. But I object on principle to restriction of my freedom of choice.'

Then there is the question of mixed marriages. Archbishop Simms put the point delicately in his interview :

'Many of our people are concerned about the marriage regulations—you know, in connexion with mixed marriages. We would like to see if there was any way in which something positive could be said, not just to bring a relaxation, but perhaps to bring more understanding into this matter'.

Other Protestants put the point more forcefully. Mr Viney quotes Dr Kenneth Milne, an officer of the General Synod of the Church of Ireland, as saying 'I object to *Ne Temere*, not because it affects us numerically, but because it strikes at the very root of family life. I would almost go so far as to suggest that it is contrary to the spirit, if not the letter, of the basic human rights.'

What most upset Mr Viney's informants, however, was the apparent capriciousness of the Catholic bureaucratic machine—the fact that a dispensation will be granted in one case and refused in another, although the circumstances appear identical. Differences between dioceses seem important here.

A result of this is that, in the Republic of Ireland, Protestant Church authorities seem even more opposed to mixed marriages than Catholic ones. They organize social occasions from which Catholics are excluded. This sets up barriers to the integration of the two communities in Ireland. But, as one Church of Ireland bishop said to Mr Viney :

'I defend the all-Protestant dance absolutely. We just must have some occasions on which young people of our Church can be sure of the faith of all the people they meet. If you want to call these dances marriage-marts, I can't argue.'

Indeed, it is very likely that even if there were no *Ne Temere* decree, church-going Protestants, in Ireland as elsewhere, would discourage their children from mixed marriages.

In Northern Ireland[2]

For a decade, until this year, relations between Northern Ireland's 900,000 Protestants and 500,000 Catholics were steadily improving. True, a great deal remained to be achieved—the removal of the discrimination against Catholics in jobs and house-allocations; the ending of the blatant gerrymandering which ensures Protestant majorities on local councils even in mainly Catholic areas; the abolition of plural votes designed to achieve the same end. But the bitter feuds of the twenties and thirties of this century, when riots and pogroms were common, seemed to have died out.

This year a new force pushed itself to the forefront. It is a form of militant Protestantism, led by a forty year old minister who founded the breakaway Free Presbyterian Church, with some three thousand members. It was this man—the Rev. Ian Paisley —who demonstrated in Rome against Archbishop Ramsey's visit to the Pope and against a sermon by a Jesuit in Westminster Abbey. In Northern Ireland he has been campaigning against the ecumenical trends of the WCC, denouncing Protestant ministers who invite priests to their presbyteries, and Protestant bishops for 'selling out to Rome'.

Since politics are inextricably linked with religion in Northern Ireland (which is constitutionally a part of the United Kingdom), he has been protesting too against the moves to improve relations between the two parts of Ireland. He has condemned as a traitor his own prime minister Captain Terence O'Neill, for his two meetings with Mr Seán Lemass, prime minister of the Republic.

[2] September-October 1966.

He condemns the new Anglo-Irish Free Trade Area agreement and the moves to bring Britain and Ireland into the European Common Market.

Anywhere else, Paisley would be ignored as an anachronism. But he is a good demagogue and he is appealing to emotions built up over three centuries of sectarian bitterness. Extremism is never far beneath the surface in Northern Ireland. The militantly republican IRA has only recently abandoned its campaign of attacks along the border between the North and the Republic. And the Northern Ireland Unionist Party, which holds a world record for being in power since the State was formed in 1922, has always depended at election time on whipping up the old passions.

Following incidents involving Queen Elizabeth when she was visiting Belfast—a bottle and a concrete block being thrown at the royal car—it was feared that sectarian violence would break out on 12 July, the day on which Northern Ireland's Protestants commemorate the historic defeat of the Catholic cause in Ireland, when William of Orange defeated James II at the Battle of the Boyne. Though this battle was fought in 1690, it is remembered in Northern Ireland as if it had taken place last week. In the event, the big demonstrations went off peacefully. Alarmed by the threat of a split in their own ranks because of the Paisley campaign, the Unionist Party and the Orange Order, twin pillars of the Northern Ireland establishment, joined forces to condemn extremism.

But at the nineteen major rallies a strongly anti-ecumenical resolution was passed. This condemned 'the present trend towards one united Church . . . the surrender of our distinctive Protestant witness . . . the compromising implications of the successive visits to the Vatican . . . marked departures within the churches from the Protestant and Reformed Faith'. This showed that Paisley's anti-ecumenism is widely supported in Northern Ireland where the WCC (because of the membership of the Orthodox Churches) and the Archbishop of Canterbury are seen as Trojan Horses about to capture 'real' Protestantism for Rome.

On 18 July Paisley and some of his clerical lieutenants were charged with causing public disturbances. Rather than pay his thirty pound fine, he went to jail.

While Paisleyism has probably been discredited as a political force, it seems clear that his anti-ecumenical clarion call has awakened the latent fears in Northern Ireland Protestantism. The realization that ecumenism does not mean a surrender to Rome will probably grow slowly. (The WCC could well consider a publicity campaign in Northern Ireland to explain what ecumenism means and its own role in the Christian Unity movement.)

5

THE LEGION OF MARY—
ITS SPIRITUALITY, METHODS
AND AIMS[1]

The Legion of Mary is probably the largest organized movement of the lay apostolate in the world. It is a lay-founded and lay-directed association which originated in Ireland in 1921. Unfortunately the Legion cannot provide exact membership figures, but it is at work in more than thirteen hundred dioceses throughout the five continents. Its official handbook is now published in thirty-one languages, and five translations are under way. Legion prayers are recited daily in approximately a hundred and twenty-five languages and dialects.

Membership is open to men and women of all standards of education and literacy, the only Legion requirements being that candidates 'lead edifying lives', have, or wish to have, the 'Legion spirit', and undertake to keep the rules. Where members cannot read or write, the essential prayers are memorized. The Legion aims at sanctifying its members by prayer and active work. Its aim and method are based on two doctrines much discussed to-day, that of the mystical body of Christ and that of Mary, mediatress of all graces. The Legion has more coloured than white members.

It came to life quietly in Dublin on 7 September 1921, during a troubled period of Irish history. The first unit, or *praesidium*, developed from a conference of the Society of St Vincent de Paul. The story is told by John Murray in a pamphlet, *Symposium on the Legion of Mary*, published in Dublin in 1958. A group of men and women, all connected with the Society, were in the habit of meeting on Sundays at Myra House, Francis Street,

[1] April 1966.

Dublin, for informal discussion of various activities. At a series of these meetings Frank Duff, a young civil servant, had talked about the 'Treatise on the True Devotion to the Blessed Virgin' by St Louis Grignon de Montfort. The Legion evolved when some of the women wished to visit the wards of the South Dublin Union hospital, and a special meeting was held to organize their work. They met on 7 September 1921, fifteen women, most of them in their late teens or early twenties, all workers, and two men, Frank Duff and Fr Michael Toher, curate at St Nicholas of Myra, Francis Street, Dublin.

Frank Duff thinks the movement was slow in growing:

'In the first year it gained four branches, and in five years it counted only nine. It took six years to give a second diocese; seven to give a second country; eight to give the first men's *praesidium*; and ten for the first branch in the New World. That was the dawning: and even then the sun seemed painfully slow in coming.'

But to the outside observer the progress hardly seems slow. Within a year of its foundation the new 'Association of Our Lady of Mercy', as it first called itself, had had a successful encounter with organized prostitution in Dublin, and had opened its first hostel for street girls. The story is told by Frank Duff in *Miracles on Tap*, published in New York in 1961, and makes exciting reading. In 1925 the name was changed to the 'Legion of Mary', and titles taken from the Roman Legion and the Roman Empire were given to all parts of the Legion organization. In 1927 the Morning Star hostel for destitute men was opened on the opposite side of the city, and was followed by Regina Coeli for women. Their story is told by Cecily Hallack in her book *The Legion of Mary*.

These early adventures were dramatic, but the methods used were identical with those of Legion precept and practice today. There was no public campaign or attempt to incriminate anyone. The street girls, and anyone else involved who permitted it, were individually approached in the effort to persuade them to give up their present way of life. The hostel was needed to give those who responded a refuge and new starting base.

This unobtrusive personal approach is the essence of Legion method as laid down in the official handbook, which gives a detailed description of the spirit and organization of the Legion and is given a unique flavour by the highly individual prose style of Frank Duff.

'The object of the Legion of Mary', says the handbook, 'is the sanctification of its members by prayer and active coopera-tion, under ecclesiastical guidance, in Mary's and the Church's work of crushing the head of the serpent and advancing the reign of Christ.

'Subject to the approval of the Concilium and to the restric-tions specified in the official Handbook of the Legion, the Legion of Mary is at the disposal of the bishop of the diocese and the parish priest for any and every form of social service and catholic action which these authorities may deem suitable to the Legionaries and useful for the welfare of the Church. Legionaries will never engage in any of these services whatso-ever in a parish without the sanction of the parish priest or of the ordinary.'

No *praesidium*, the basic local unit of the Legion, may be established without permission from the Concilium, the central governing body in Dublin, or from a Curia or Senatus, regional councils subordinate to the Concilium. The permission of the parish priest or ordinary is also needed. The Concilium consists of representatives of all Legionary bodies directly related to itself, and the members of the Dublin Curia, with a spiritual director appointed by the Irish bishops.

The *praesidium* is composed of from four to twenty or more members, men or women, or both, with a president, vice-presi-dent, secretary, and treasurer appointed by its immediately superior council, and a spiritual director appointed by the parish priest. The *praesidium* meets weekly, an inviolable rule, and the order of its meeting is laid down in detail, largely based on St Vincent de Paul procedure. It begins and ends with prayer, and pauses midway for further prayer and a short spiritual talk.

C

Minutes are read and signed, verbal reports on work done are given, and work for the coming week is allocated. Attendance at this weekly meeting, the 'power-house' and 'heart' of the Legion as the handbook calls it, is the primary obligation of the member. The Standing Instruction, read aloud once a month at the *praesidium* meeting, states :

'Legionary duty requires from each Legionary :

'First, the punctual and regular attendance at the weekly meetings of the *praesidium* and the furnishing there of an adequate and audible report on the work done;

'Second, the daily recitation of the Catena;

'Third, the performance of a substantial active Legionary work, in the spirit of faith, and in union with Mary, in such fashion that in those worked for and in one's fellow-members, the person of our Lord is once again seen and served by Mary, his Mother;

'Fourth, the preservation of an absolute secrecy in regard to any matter discussed at the meeting or learned in connection with the Legionary work.'

At the weekly meeting the two weapons of prayer and work fuse, for the Legion sees them as mutually dependent for their respective growth.

The Legion 'places before its members a mode of life rather than the doing of a work. It provides an intensely ordered system, in which much is given the force of rule that in other systems is merely exhorted or left to be understood', and it judges perfection of membership by 'exact adherence to its system', rather than by apparent success. Therefore it encourages its members to refuse 'to accept defeat, or to court it by a tendency to grade items of work in terms of the "promising", the "unpromising", the "hopeless", etc', and is 'concerned only in a secondary way about a programme of works, but much about intensity of purpose'.

Specified works are not laid down, but those chosen should be directed to 'actual needs, and amongst the latter, towards the gravest'. The one prohibition is the giving of material relief. It 'may be to other societies a key which opens. It is the key with which the Legion locks itself out.' The Legion's apostolate is directed to literally every individual, and material help would put it on a false footing with many.

House to house visitation by legionaries in pairs is one of the most characteristic of legionary works. It can be undertaken for various proximate ends, parish census taking, sale of Catholic papers and so on. This must be done

'quietly, unobtrusively, delicately. It aims less at the direct suppressing of gross evils than at the permeation of the community with Catholic principles and Catholic feeling, so that the evils die of themselves through lack of a soil favourable to them.'

This is why the Legion does not take part in public campaigns of any kind, since that might compromise its real work with the individual. Hostels, clubs, study groups, book-barrows, catechetics —the works of the Legion are innumerable, but all are based on the idea of the individual communicating with the individual.

The Legion believes that every Catholic, by virtue of his baptism and membership of the mystical body of Christ, has a duty to try to spread his faith, and quotes in support the words of Popes Pius X, Pius XI, and Pius XII. The Legion further argues that since all have the duty, almost all must be capable of responding, and hence that no high degree of education or mental ability, however welcome, is essential. The average Catholic, the Legion believes, knows more about his religion than he or others realize, and most questioners want to know what Catholics believe, not why, so that a simple explanation of Catholic belief is often all that is needed. To those who fear indiscretions and blunders the Handbook answers that prudence should be the 'brake' but not the 'engine' and, ready as always with a quotation, quotes Newman that 'to do some substantial good is the compensation for much incidental imperfection', and also Bossuet's recommendation that, 'when considering her [Mary], speak not . . . of human rules . . . tell of the rules of God'.

The Legion believes that for many its highly organized system will be the best means of answering their call to the apostolate and developing their full potential. It believes that all things are possible to faith and hard work, and constantly emphasizes the need to aim high.

'Nothing can stand in the way of success except want of trust. If there be but faith enough, God will utilize us to conquer the world for Him.'

The Handbook gives a glimpse of the ultimate ideal :

'Suppose a nation were to arise, which built its life on lofty standards, and held up to the world the example of a whole people putting its faith into practice, and hence, as a matter of course, solving its problems.'

This whole system of prayer and work is given its distinctive legionary character by the Legion's reliance on Mary, mediatress of all graces. Mary, says the Handbook, is one of God's creatures, and is 'far more than any others—His creature, because He has wrought more in her than in any other of His creatures'. He has chosen to redeem man through her, and to ask her permission to do this. By her fiat to the annunciation Mary became the channel through which all grace comes to us. Cardinal Suenens, in his book on *The Theology of the Apostolate of the Legion of Mary*, asks whether the birth of Jesus through Mary was 'merely a remote historical fact, complete in itself? Or do these words open up for us and for all future time an unchanging law of God's action in the world?'

The Legion feels it is logical to conclude in view of Mary's position that 'in union with her we approach him more effectively, and hence win grace more freely'. 'Incessantly must the Legionary dwell upon the reality of Mary's motherhood of us.'

The legionary promise, which is made by each member at a *praesidium* meeting after three months probation, sums up both the theology and the spirit of the Legion.

'Most Holy Spirit, I, . . .
Desiring to be enrolled this day as a Legionary of Mary,
Yet knowing that of myself I cannot render worthy service,

Do ask thee to come upon me and fill me with thyself,

So that my poor acts may be sustained by thy power, and become an instrument of thy mighty purposes.

But I know that thou, who hast come to regenerate the world in Jesus Christ,

Hast not willed to do so except through Mary;

That without her we cannot know or love thee;

That it is by her, and to whom she pleases, when she pleases, and in the quantity and manner she pleases,

That all thy gifts and virtues and graces are administered;

And I realize that the secret of a perfect Legionary service

Consists in a complete union with her who is so completely united to thee,

So, taking in my hand the Legionary Standard, which seeks to set before our eyes these things,

I stand before thee as her soldier and her child,

And I so declare my entire dependence on her.

She is the mother of my soul.

Her heart and mine are one;

And from that single heart she speaks again those words of old :

"Behold the handmaid of the Lord";

And once again thou comest by her to do great things.

Let thy power overshadow me, and come into my soul with fire and love

And make it one with Mary's love and Mary's will to save the world;

So that I may be pure in her who was made immaculate by thee;

So that Christ my Lord may likewise grow in me through thee;

So that I with her, his Mother, may bring him to the world and to the souls who need him;

So that they and I, the battle won, may reign with her for ever in the glory of the Blessed Trinity.

Confident that thou wilt so receive me—and use me—and turn my weakness into strength this day,

I take my place in the ranks of the Legion, and I venture to promise a faithful service.

I will submit fully to its discipline,

Which binds me to my comrades,
And shapes us to an army,
And keeps our line as we march on with Mary,
To work thy will, to operate thy miracles of grace,
Which will renew the face of the earth,
And establish thy reign, most Holy Spirit, over all.
In the name of the Father and of the Son and of the Holy
   Ghost, Amen.'

This is a generous statement of belief and intention, but one
phrase has troubled people attracted by the Legion. Is it 'by her,
and to whom she pleases, and in the quantity and manner she
pleases', that all his gifts and virtues and graces are administered?
The logical implication of this phrase seems to be an arbitrary
right of choice on Mary's part which, they think, goes beyond
the officially approved belief of some Catholics that all grace
actually comes through Mary.

The close connection between the Legion of Mary and the
'Treatise on the True Devotion to the Blessed Virgin', by St
Louis Grignon de Montfort, causes same Catholics to view the
former with a certain suspicion, on the grounds that St Louis
carried the Marian cult to undesirable lengths. The Legion does
not insist that its members adopt de Montfort's way but does
recommend it to them, and the Handbook acknowledges the
Legion's debt to the saint; its prayers 'echo his words', and he is
'really the tutor of the Legion'.

St Louis was born in Brittany in 1673 and died in 1716. He
spent his life as a missioner and founded two orders, one of nuns
and one of priests. The treatise was written early in the eighteenth
century but remained in manuscript until found in 1842 at the
Monfortian mother house in Vendée. It was published and an
English translation appeared in 1862. After some initial doubt at
Rome the treatise was explicitly approved by Popes Pius X and
Benedict XV, and then by Pius XII, who canonized the saint in
1947, and termed the Treatise 'flagrans, solida, et recta'.

Dr Donal Flanagan, professor of dogmatic theology at Maynooth, has stated that de Montfort's method of total dependence
on Mary was not an 'unbalanced spirituality; it was rather the

corollary of a deeply held theological conviction of the divinely
ordained place and role of Mary in the salvation of man'.

De Montfort admitted that his method of devotion, which he
claimed to be of ancient origin, had met criticism throughout its
history. Since its rediscovery in 1842 it was viewed with initial
suspicion at Rome, though it has since been triumphantly vindicated there. The theological basis of the devotion, i.e. de Montfort's assessment of Mary's part in the redemption, is not questioned by theologians. Yet it is a fact that his conclusions—that
our best way to Jesus is through Mary—causes some Catholics to
feel uneasy.

This brings us to an allied point. Today when we stress the
respect due to the beliefs of others and the possibility of learning
much that is of value from Orthodox and Protestants and from
other world religions such as Hinduism, Buddhism, and Islam,
there is a tendency to lay less emphasis on those aspects of
Christianity and Catholicism that are controversial. Here the
Legion, as a leading example of Marian cult, is at the centre of
the discussion.

Which is the true charity: to put aside as far as possible for
the time being those subjects on which we differ, and concentrate on finding out how far we agree and on exploring the beliefs
of others, as is being done with exciting results—or to try to reformulate the controversial beliefs in language which will make
them intelligible to those who might not be so opposed if they
understood exactly the disputed doctrines and their history in
Christian belief? The answer would seem to be that the two
approaches are not contradictory but complementary, and the
Legion would claim that it is not true charity to play down
Mary's role if we really believe in it, and can point to the fact
that the Catholic Church has proclaimed its belief in the lasting
significance of Mary's part in the redemption by the approval of
the feast of Mary, mediatress of all graces, and by the dogmas of
the immaculate conception and the assumption.

The uneasiness caused to some by the Montfortian way and
the emphasis on Mary's role is understandable; it includes a belief that at least some devotees of Mary lose sight of Jesus by their

emphasis on his mother, and a fear of a threat to the infinite variety of religious experience. Perhaps there is need for better communications, and the Legion might benefit everyone by publicizing the theological basis of its devotion to Mary.

Difficulties of another kind for the Legion were caused by the 'Catholic Action' movement originated by Pope Pius XI. Ireland was little affected, but elsewhere, especially on the continent of Europe, the Legion feels that its progress was at least slowed down. It did not enter France until 1940, Germany until 1944, Belgium and Luxemburg until 1945, Italy and Switzerland until 1946, Denmark until 1948, Austria and Portugal until 1949, and Spain until 1950, though in the meantime it had reached North and Central America, Africa and Asia, Australia, New Zealand, and the West Indies.

Dr Jeremiah Newman, professor of Catholic Sociology and Catholic Action at Maynooth, has written a book, *What is Catholic Action?*, published in 1958, which explains the position. The trouble started simply enough with Pope Pius XI's call for the 'participation of the laity in the apostolate of the Church's hierarchy'. This he called 'Catholic Action' and usually limited the use of this term to describe, in Dr Newman's words, 'apostolic activity carried on by organizations of the laity for the assistance of the hierarchy, at the special mandate of the hierarchy and in direct dependence on it'. This led to considerable difference of opinion as to what exactly was or was not a mandate, and as to the relative standing of the new 'Catholic Action' movements and of existing organizations such as the Legion of Mary which were highly organized and apostolic but independent of the hierarchy.

The dispute extended to include the proper sphere of lay activity in the Church and relations between clergy and laity. Mgr Gerard Philips, professor of dogmatic theology at Louvain, in his book *The Role of the Laity in the Church*, admits that the 'very mention of this name [Catholic Action] immediately evokes all the thorny problems surrounding the hierarchy and the laity and often involves heated arguments'.

The real danger, as Dr Newman points out, was that 'the field of apostolic activity and action will . . . tend to be reserved to a certain type of mandated organization, calling itself "Catholic Action", to the exclusion of all other types'. He also thinks that in missionary countries 'there may have been a tendency to confine the apostolic field to a restricted system of "Catholic Action" conceived along rather narrow lines'.

The difficulties that arose were real enough for Pope Pius XII to raise the question before the Second World Congress of the Lay Apostolate in 1957. It had been suggested, he said, that the use of the term 'Catholic Action' led to the idea of a 'monopoly' and 'exclusivism', and it had been proposed to give back to the term 'its general meaning . . . of lay apostolic movements, organized and recognized as such'.

In a later book, *The Christian in Society*, Dr Newman traces the oscillating relations of clergy and laity throughout the history of the Church, and concludes that the chief difficulty is the lack of a theology of the layman. In this respect, Vatican II has made no more than a beginning.

On the other hand, the 'lay' nature of the Legion and its relationship to the clergy at parish level is somewhat ambiguous. There is such a thing as a 'clericalist' laity, and the Legion often seems to attract this kind of people. Its ethos does not seem to lend itself to producing a truly 'secular Christianity'—to christianizing secular values and life. Every parish group has, theoretically at least, a 'spiritual director' drawn from the parish clergy, and it is considered good Legion spirit to place the parish group at the disposal of the parish priest. Sometimes the Legion parish group exists almost on sufferance, as far as the clergy are concerned. At other times, due perhaps to local circumstances or to the character of the priest in question, the spiritual director can become *de facto* the director of a *praesidium's* activities.

The Legion of Mary has spread over the five continents. At first the growth was spontaneous. Often a priest or bishop became interested in what he saw or heard of the Legion and asked to have it introduced into his parish or diocese. In 1934 the Legion inaugurated its own system of extension, the Legion envoyship. An envoy is a lay member who serves abroad for a period usually of three years, extending and organizing the Legion in his allotted territory and then returns to his former occupation.

Since 1934, sixty-six envoys have been sent all over the world, most but not all of them Irish. The most famous is undoubtedly Edel Quinn, whose biography has been written by Cardinal Suenens. She was a frail girl, rejected for the religious life because of tuberculosis, but she worked in East Africa, establishing the Legion all over the huge areas of Kenya, Tanganyika, Nyasaland, Uganda, Zanzibar, and Mauritius, for seven and a half years until her death in Nairobi in 1944. The first step towards her beatification has been taken.

The impression she made on those who met her did incalculable service in building an international reputation for the Legion, and the fact that she was allowed to go to Africa at all on such work highlights a characteristic of the Legion and of Frank Duff that is rare enough today : the courage sometimes to do what is rash by human standards. By any human standards a girl in Edel Quinn's state of health should not have been sent to Africa on envoy work. She wanted to go, and Frank Duff agreed that she should and persuaded the Concilium to sanction her envoyship. She went, and it is hard to say where the results of her going will end.

One of the people Edel Quinn impressed was Mgr Riberi, then apostolic delegate in East Africa and later papal internuncio in China. In 1948 he asked Fr Aedan McGrath of the Columban Mission to China to try to spread the Legion of Mary there.

It had been introduced into China in 1937 but had not made much headway. Now it began to spread so rapidly that the Concilium remonstrated with Fr McGrath, fearing that this mushroom growth might prove ephemeral. But instead the Legion now feels that its history in China has proved its quality and, in Frank Duff's words, has been 'the Legionary glory'.

Since the last missionaries were expelled from China news is hard to get. A book by a French Jesuit Fr Jean Monsterleet, who worked in China, published in an English translation in 1956 as *Martyrs in China*, gives a picture of the Church in China to that date, and his testimony as to the Legion is the more impressive since he is concerned with the Church as a whole and only incidentally with the Legion. He praises the achievement of Catholic Action before 1948 in ridding Chinese Christians of the 'ghetto mentality', but is explicit that the 'most important event in the history of the lay apostolate (in China) was the advent of the Legion of Mary in 1948'.

After the communist takeover there was an attempt to create patriotic Chinese Christian churches by expelling the foreigners and persuading the Chinese Christians to denounce them as imperialists and the Catholics to renounce Rome. The Chinese Catholics as a body refused to do so, and Legionaries were prominent in stiffening the resistance; they were so prominent that a stock question to suspects, as a loyalty test, became : did they consider the Legion of Mary to be a 'reactionary, imperialistic organization'?

Persecution intensified : schools, universities, churches, and hospitals were taken over, Mgr Riberi was expelled, foreign and Chinese priests were imprisoned, often tortured, and the former finally expelled. The three thousand foreign priests in China in 1948 had dwindled to thirty by June 1955. The Legion of Mary, says Fr Monsterleet, was 'the target of a particularly violent campaign'; many members were imprisoned and some are known to have been executed. The full story will not be told for some time to come.

The Legion is proud of its Chinese members and proud to have been singled out for special attention by the Communists.

The spread of the Legion beyond the faithful of the Latin-rite Church confronted it with some problems which put a strain on its established devotional structure. In an article on the rosary in the December 1965 number of *Maria Legionis*, Frank Duff tells how one of these problems was solved :

> 'When the Legion began to grow among the Uniates, and after that among the Orthodox or non-united section, the problem of replacing the rosary by some other prayer had to be faced up to. Why not, you might say, press the rosary upon them? Well, Rome had asked us not to do that, not to latinize them. So we had to seek for a substitute. The efforts which were

made in that direction have important bearing. The tale is too long to tell here. It suffices to say that every expedient was tried and failed until at last the Uniate Greeks helped us out by a compromise. I give you the solution.

'They adopted a sort of rosary which contained 7 of our 15 mysteries. Each of those mysteries was preluded by a little introduction or meditation, followed by one Pater, three Aves and one Gloria. In other words, the whole contained 7 preludes, 7 Paters, 21 Aves, 7 Glorias, these being followed by the remainder of the Legion prayers. It has been a success. It produces the same conditions and tone as our rosary, thus endorsing the rosary and also showing how hard it is to replace it.'

The Legion of Mary has 'arrived': are we any nearer to an understanding of what it is? The Legion aims at the sanctification of its members by prayer and active work for the sanctification of their fellowmen, so that it aims at the spiritual development of the whole community. It has chosen to pray and work in closest union with Mary as the best and easiest way of becoming united with God. Next, it may be noted that doctrinally it is very much a twentieth-century movement. Fr Donnchadh Ó Floinn, Spiritual Director to the Concilium, says:

'It is so much a product of its time that it is not easy to see how it could have existed even a few years before it actually began. The Catholic truths that gave it its special structure received attention from those popes under whom it has lived. It was Benedict XV who approved the proper Mass and office of our Lady, mediatress of all graces. Pius XI was the pope of the lay apostolate. During the pontificate of Pius XII the doctrine of the mystical body has been illumined by official teaching and by deep study.'

The Legion really anticipates that someday it will 'conquer the world'. 'Is it fantastic', asks Frank Duff, apropos of the Legion in China, to see the Legion as 'a supreme hope of the Church, an army in battle-array against the hostile forces of the world? . . . There has to be a proportion between the past and the future.'

The Legion thinks big. And this is good psychology. Fr Ó Floinn points out :

'One reason why the Legion is such a sturdy growth is that it demands heroism from quite ordinary people who would be repelled by a stystem that put up with mediocrity.'

Frank Duff says that the membership of the Legion is 'just common, human material, typical, and weak'. The Legion does not seek to recruit an élite. It aims to create one from this ordinary material. The sound of the trumpet calling to a holy war is hard to resist, and when it is backed by a highly organized system that keeps the recruit constantly in action and reinforces his morale at every point, then perhaps as good a formula as any has been found for maintaining enthusiasm and performance. In countries where education is limited or lacking it has been noted that Legion membership and especially attendance at the weekly *praesidium* meeting, with its ordered agenda of prayer, minutes, reports, allocation of new works, has an educative value in itself.

However, since the avowed aim of the Legion is the spiritual penetration of the entire community, it is permissable to ask how far in any given community this has been achieved. Has the penetration in depth and height kept pace with the horizontal—geographical—extension around the world? If it had, this would certainly be apparent by now, at the very least in the Legion's country of origin, or in the British Isles as a whole. But it is not apparent. In university and professional circles, in the political milieu and in fashionable society, the Legion has not been able to make its mark. To a great degree its members seem to lack the qualities of mind, of personality, or of both, which are necessary for effective participation in these central areas; the legionaries project an image of the Legion which fails to attract people who value such qualities.

There could be several explanations for this defective range of influence. Does the Legion stress one-sidedly the role of supernatural grace in the apostolate to the neglect of the role which human qualities can play—natural grace and vitality, mental qualities, charm, elegance? Does the Legion prefer to work with certain kinds of human beings—or is there no such preference and has something simply gone wrong?

The family is another sphere, cutting across the spheres just mentioned, in which it is not apparent that the Legion is as effective as it might be. There are many *praesidia* where it is accepted as normal or inevitable that a girl member, on marrying, leaves the Legion. This may conceivably be one reason why the Legion, in Europe at least, is not associated in people's minds with attractive and fulfilled marriage or family life. Even persons who appreciate the Legion's work feel that there is something vaguely 'old-maidish' about it—nor would they ascribe this impression exclusively to their experience of women legionaries.

The place of Mary in the Church, the role of the layman, the relation of the Catholic Church to other Christian churches and to other religions—all vitally concern the Legion. Its attitudes to all that concerns it are very definite and therefore it arouses disapproval as well as approval.

The latest sign of papal encouragement was a letter which Mr Duff received in January 1965 from Cardinal Cicognani. It conveyed the Pope's 'praise and encouragement' to the Legion, and noted the

> 'spirit of the Legion of Mary, [which] while properly drawing fruitful nourishment from the strong interior life of its members, from their discipline, their dedication to the salvation of their neighbour, their unflinching loyalty to the Church, nevertheless is distinguished and characterized by an adamant confidence in the action of the Blessed Virgin.'

Since then Frank Duff has become the first Irishman to be invited as a lay observer to the Vatican Council.

6

FIRST FRUITS OF THE COUNCIL

Liturgy Reform[1]

The vernacular Mass and the other changes laid down in the Instruction for implementing the Liturgy Constitution were introduced simultaneously at the beginning of Lent this year. The work of preparatory instruction had got under way early. Special efforts were made in the Munster dioceses. In their Lenten pastorals most of the Irish bishops dealt in detail with the liturgical changes. Some of them acknowledged that it would take time to become accustomed to the radical revision in the manner of celebrating Mass; others asked for clear, loud responses from the faithful in the body of the church.

An example of the kind of work done to prepare the people for the reforms and to give them a better understanding of the liturgy was the eight-page document *The New Constitution on the Liturgy*, issued to priests by the Diocesan Commissions of Limerick and Killaloe (quoted in *The Furrow*, October 1964). Its object was to outline twelve sermons to be preached from 27 September to 4 December on the new Constitution. The sermon notes were intended to direct the priest's preparatory study of the subject. They were accompanied by specific references to relevant lessons in the German Catholic Catechism. The 'Hints for the Effective Use of the Programme' were as follows:

1. Use language as simple, concrete and scriptural as in the Constitution.
2. Whatever is said should be related to what the people know and enlivened with illustrations drawn from contemporary events and common experience.

[1] April 1965.

79

3. As far as possible present the matter, as Christ did, in narrative, direct, or other interesting form.

The fundamental theme of the sermons was 'The Mystery of Christ'. The twelve themes were as follows :

1. Contact with the person of Christ.
2. The story of Christ's coming to save mankind—his preaching and healing the contrite of heart.
3. Christ the perfect man—his love and obedience to his Father climaxed in his passion, resurrection, and glorification.
4. The Church is Christ.
5. The liturgy is the principal activity of the Church.
6. The Mass—the new and eternal covenant.
7. The Mass one single act of worship.
8. The sacraments are closely linked with the Mass and the paschal mystery.
9. Our personal response to Christ.
10. The Lord's Day and the community celebrations of the people of God.
11. Liturgy and Christian life.
12. Preparing to live with Christ for ever.

The 'Latinity' of Catholicism is obviously not a fetish of any substantial body of Irish Catholics. The vernacular Mass has been welcomed enthusiastically or else accepted passively. There was no vocal opposition. Any reluctance was the reluctance of people to change a state of affairs in which even mute attendance at Mass was, for the average Irishman, something deeply satisfying and of enormous importance. When the late Brendan Behan once dismissed one of his television appearances with the words 'It's not something important, it's not like going to Mass', he was saying something that made profound sense to him as an Irish Catholic, and to the average Irish Catholic. What reluctance there was on the part of Irish priests and people was a compound of two things : lack of awareness of the need to change and fear of the unknown, of what might harm something deeply valued. When the new liturgy was seen and heard and when people had a chance to take part in it, the fears of many vanished and gave way to delighted surprise.

English versions of the scriptures approved for use in Ireland are the Douay, the Confraternity of Christian Doctrine (American), Boylan, and the version of the St Andrew Bible Missal. Four Irish-language versions of the scriptures are also approved for use. Regulations for the use of the English and Irish vernaculars vary somewhat from diocese to diocese. While a vernacular language is obligatory at all Masses at high altars on Sundays and holidays of obligation throughout the country, Latin is obligatory at weekday Masses in many dioceses. In every diocese some provision is made for Sunday Masses in Irish—for example, one each Sunday at the high altar of each parish church in the Dublin archdiocese. In the small Irish-speaking districts of the country the vernacular Masses are in Irish.

On 7 March, Cardinal William Conway, Archbishop of Armagh and Primate of All Ireland, celebrated the first Mass in Irish at the Franciscan College, Gormanston, which was attended by a distinguished gathering led by President Eamon de Valera. The Mass was televised by Telefis Eireann.

An Irish Theological Association[2]

Publishers' lists are notably short on books by Irish theologians. Irish theologians made little significant contribution to the proceeding of Vatican II. In the field of communications in Ireland theology has found few articulate voices. TV discussions week by week brought no promising theological publicist to the attention of the Irish public, Seán MacRéamoinn's television and radio reporting from Rome still shines by its splendid isolation in that medium.

There may be considerable significance attaching to the news that an Irish Theological Association is in process of being formed and that it held its inaugural meeting at St Patrick's College, Carlow (the doyen of the Irish seminaries) early in January. The new society proposes to study and discuss matters of particular interest to teachers of theology. The January conference theme,

[2] February 1966.

'Vatican II and the Teaching of Theology', identified the organization with the programme for renewal sanctioned in St Peter's.

Hitherto the Irish seminaries have been severely practical in
outlook and training. They were content to leave the pursuit of
scholarship to Maynooth, the national seminary, while the other
six regional seminaries trained a pastoral clergy. Clonliffe College,
Dublin, is the only diocesan seminary in Ireland catering for the
growing needs of the capital. Seminaries at Waterford, Kilkenny,
Thurles, Carlow and the Dublin missionary seminary, All Hal-
lows, are concerned in the main with furnishing priests to under-
staffed dioceses of the English-speaking world. In estimating the
contribution of these colleges to theology one must judge more
from the standards of pastoral effectiveness than from the
scholarly writings which have emerged.

In all cases the seminaries are crowded with seminarians but
short on professors. Resources are pitifully inadequate to do
anything more than maintain the buildings. Library facilities are
poor. There are no endowments and too little leisure to enable
professors to specialize or develop special lines of interest. Relevant to the theme of the January conference is the lack of
facilities for the pedagogical formation of seminary staff.

It is curious to reflect that the January meeting brought together for the first time from a score of theologates, men who have
been doing professional work over the years without ever ex-
changing experiences, comparing methods, or pooling resources.
The rugged individualism that maintains so many theologates
for religious in Ireland is bound to come under examination at a
moment when the Church cannot spare priests from the pastoral
ministry.

The advantages of a unified seminary policy in applying the
decrees of the Council on the training of priests are obvious. The
real renewal begins with clergy who are thoroughly committed.
The lessons of Trent are clear. The seminary is the kingpin of
reform. It remains to be seen if the new generation of seminary
professors can snap out of the isolation which has up to now
diminished their effective contribution to the Church and nation.

Theology is esteemed and admired in Ireland but regarded as
a highly specialized study outside the range of everyman's

interests. Pastoral practice has emphasized sacramental and devotional expression at the expense of doctrinal training. There is no university faculty of Catholic theology. After referring to the advantages with which the Church of the aggiornamento can reckon in Ireland, an editorial writer in the December number of *Hibernia* stated that these are 'offset' by our lack of advanced religious education and its counterpart, our weakness in theology, and went on to say :

'It should not any longer be necessary to prove the desirability and necessity of theological education for university people, still less its necessity for sisters, brothers, and lay teachers on whom so much of the religious education of our young people depends.'

Theology has become more fluent since 1950. What *The Furrow* has done well at the level of pastoral application, the *Irish Theological Quarterly* is doing at a high scholarly level. Theological writing in Britain has always had the advantage of a more literary and jargon-free medium of expression. Is this due to the absence of challenge in the Irish seminary climate and the absence of dialogue with Protestant schools of theology? Ireland, famed for her writers, is sadly lacking in theologians with a flair for language.

The foundation of the Irish Theological Association is a timely expression of the concern of the Church to communicate the good news to modern man in today's idiom and in the way best calculated to serve the Church through the world. Modernization in this case means adaptation to the highest standards of professional competence which alone can ensure pastoral effectiveness. In the changing religious and social circumstances of Ireland today, the clergy will be put to the pins of their collars to make their own role and their message seem directly relevant in everyday life.

'In some countries rich in vocations, like Ireland', wrote Douglas Woodruff in *The Tablet* (11 December 1965), 'the clergy will never have it quite so good again, never receive quite such a premium in authority and respect for the years of philosophical and theological study which set them intellectually apart from and above the faithful'.

There is every reason to believe that hundreds of dioceses throughout the English-speaking world will continue to depend for their supply of priests upon Ireland's seminaries. The January meeting of the theologians at Carlow could have a significant contribution to make in a wider context. But their contribution must begin at home. Not until Irish theologians and the priests who derive their theology from them have learned to speak inspiringly to their own people will they be able to speak inspiringly to anyone else.

Catholic Ireland, which is taking obediently to the new liturgy and (formally at least) to the new theology, and where enthusiasm for the new catechetical methods is widespread, is indeed one of the best examples of the fact that with the end of the Council all that is necessary for the revitalization of Catholic life in our time has by no means been done. Vocations are plentiful, the churches full, and yet a growing question-mark haunts all the vigorous activism of clergy and laity alike. The recent years of increasing affluence have to some extent unbalanced a people unused to wealth. The crass materialism and the material ugliness which became features of Irish Catholic life in the nineteenth century have taken new, more glaring forms. Not that the wealth is the trouble, nor that there is any major reluctance to spread it equitably. The trouble is that this Mass-going people seems to have little idea of how to enrich life through the power, freedom, and leisure which wealth gives—and that no powerful competing aim of a humanistic kind is effectively proposed.

Fr Andrew Farrell of Navan went right to the heart of the matter when he spoke in a sermon last December of 'the parents and educators who did not provide our young people with a challenging set of ideals—with something to strive for in life as men and women'. That was a sharp reproach in a country where the good news is preached freely and taught in every school. While needless strike after needless strike has been revealing greed, a sense of frustration, and bad management-labour relations, the Church has largely remained silent—as if it just didn't matter or was not the Church's concern. Despite some clamour for 'more participation' the educated laity seem content to remain just that —a 'laity', in the intellectually passive late Tridentine sense. They remain quite unproductive of serious Christian thought or speech about the purpose of life in general, and in particular of life in Ireland today.

Unfairly isolated by a laity who show little serious concern, and by bishops who administer rather than lead, the priest-theologians have their work cut out for them if they are to provide that inspiring vision of 'something to strive for in life as men and women' which is the only answer to the mute question-mark now nagging more urgently than before in priests and people.

A new Biblical Association[3]

Despite the remarkable devotion to the Bible in the old Irish Church, visitors to Ireland today will not find much evidence of enthusiasm for the Bible in the public religious life of Irish Catholics. The Bible is not enthroned in the churches; the insignificant and often mean lecterns, which now find place in the sanctuaries as the setting for the reading of the word of God, are the product of obedience rather than appreciation. Books on scriptural themes are not much in evidence on the presbytery bookshelves. Priests raise all kinds of difficulties against the introduction of the scriptural homily; the catechetical instructions prescribed in every diocese are the product of the era before the study of the Bible was restored to its rightful place in seminary programmes.

Ireland boasts of a faith in the scriptures which is imperishably enshrined in the Books of Kells and in the Book of Durrow. History explains why today's situation is less healthy. Irish seminaries were greatly influenced in the nineteenth century by the siege mentality of late Tridentine Catholicism in its English-speaking version. Where Protestantism in its Anglo-Saxon forms was in the ascendant, seminary emphases leaned heavily upon the doctrines of papal infallibility, the authority of the Church, and a close adherence to the united front of the manualists. Discipline,

[3] April 1966.

obedience and a thorough grounding in moral theology were the ideals proposed and accepted, with results which for a time seemed satisfactory. The manner of teaching scripture was along the pedestrian text-exegesis lines, not differing greatly from the study of Latin or Greek classical texts. In some seminaries there were no lectures devoted to the Old Testament until a decade or two ago.

Irish biblical scholarship has not had the stimulus of a mind of the stature of, say, M. J. Lagrange to initiate a school of study or a biblical movement worthy of the name. In this century the outstanding names are Cardinal Joseph Macrory, Mgr Patrick Boylan, and Mgr E. J. Kissane, authors of commentaries on St John's Gospel, St Paul's letters to the Corinthians, the Psalms, St Paul to the Romans, Isaiah, Job. There is no magazine in Ireland devoted to the exposition of the scriptures, either for popular or specialist consumption. Indeed it must be admitted that the status of scripture as a seminary subject envisaged in the code of canon law and in the instruction issued by the Biblical Commission in 1950 has not been realized in the majority of seminaries.

Certainly, the identification of British power with Protestantism, and the proselytizing efforts of the Bible societies in the famine years, contributed to the present situation. Priests formed in seminaries where the Bible was not given an outstanding place could hardly be expected to change the currents of popular devotion which were focused upon the Mass, the spiritualized person of Christ, the blessed Virgin Mary, and favourite saints. The Latin liturgy confirmed the tendency to regard the scripture as irrelevant to the spiritual life of the man in the street.

It would not be true to say that the modern biblical movement has not touched Irish Catholics, even if only in a modest way. Nuns have entered wholeheartedly into the modern catechetical movement and through it have grown to love the scriptures. Many summer schools include scriptural talks. There are study groups in some convents. The apostolate of the Bible in convents would be immensely helped forward by the cooperation of retreat masters imbued with the spirit of *Divino afflante Spiritu* and the Council documents. Parish study groups are few and far between. The recent instruction of the Congregation of Seminaries on the implementing of the Liturgy Constitution in seminaries should give a spur to scripture studies. Already some progress is reported, and many seminarians are enthusiastic recruits to the biblical movement.

Other promising initiatives have been taken. An oblate priest organizes circles of nuns who follow a scripture course which is tape-recorded and circulated every month to the participants. A seminary professor has several groups of parish clergy who follow a regular programme of Bible study under the guidance of priest-leaders who consult with him every week. The professor of Eastern languages in University College, Dublin, has four nuns among his students. He, too, conducts extra-mural courses in scripture for groups of up to a hundred. More than half of the students are nuns. The Dominican sisters now receive regular scriptural training from qualified priests during their novitiate years.

A welcome sign of possibly better things to come is the recent decision of the Irish bishops to launch a Catholic Biblical Association of Ireland:

'to foster knowledge and love of the scriptures in conformity with the teaching and instructions of the Church

to promote scientific study of the Bible and of the branches of learning connected with it;

to organize congresses, conferences, study groups, etc., and to arrange lectures on biblical subjects' (Art. 2 of Constitution).

The initiative to form the Catholic Biblical Association of Ireland came from the standing committee of the Irish hierarchy in February of 1965. It was intended to set up an organization to provide up-to-date guidance for all students of scripture and to supplement the work of existing groups, notably the Irish Biblical Association which has been functioning for ten years. A draft constitution was approved by the bishops in November 1965.

Cardinal Conway went to Maynooth on 22 February for the inaugural meeting of the association. Professors of scripture from all the seminaries and theologates were present to hear him welcome the launching of the new theological association and the new biblical society as the first fruits of the renewal prescribed by the Council. Addressing the thirty-five professors of scripture gathered at Maynooth, the Cardinal stressed the desire of all the bishops to see the newly founded societies making a substantial contribution to the development and enrichment of the sacred sciences in Ireland. The rich body of Council teaching had to be gathered, harvested, processed and distributed. He saw both societies playing a big role in the life of the Church. Sacred scripture was the fine point upon which everything else was balanced. Its study was fundamental now.

Cardinal Conway spoke of the elation felt by students of scripture in using the new tools and methods placed at their disposition. He told of how on a visit to Jerusalem last November he had received inquiries at the Ecole de St Etienne for the good health of Mgr Patrick Boylan, the grand old man of Irish biblical studies. Fittingly Mgr Boylan was unanimously elected chairman of the new body. Fr Wilfred Harrington, O.P., author of a three-volume introduction to the Bible, *Record of Revelation*, was appointed vice-chairman. Prof. John A. O'Flynn of Maynooth is secretary.

The situation is ripe for a step forward in the study and popularization of sacred scripture. There is some reluctance to face this fact.

'And yet, change we must. The future of the Church depends on it, and this is true also in our own country which is so loyal to past traditions. What happened in France (the 'eldest daughter') could conceivably happen in Ireland. Whether we like it or not, our traditional way of life is disappearing, and industrialization is coming our way. We, more than other countries, have still a chance of wedding our worship easily and gradually to the new social pattern, a chance we cannot afford to pass by' (Fr Kevin Condon, C.M.).

The field of opportunity open to the members of the new biblical society is rich. Apart from intensified scriptural training in the seminaries according to the prescriptions of the Council, there is the urgent need to train religion teachers and undertake a vast popular adult educational campaign. If the latter is neglected the interest aroused by the Council may wither and perish.

The provision of a centre for biblical studies in Ireland is likely to be among the projects to engage the attention of the new association.

Reform of Religious Instruction[4]

On 29 September 1966, Cardinal Conway was 'The Person in Question' in an Irish television programme which goes by that title. Questioned by a panel of young people about Ireland after the Council, the Cardinal pointed to the new direction of seminary training at Maynooth as one focal point for a renewal of the Church in Ireland. Another sign of significant aggiornamento, he said, was the introduction of a new syllabus of religious instruction in the secondary schools.

This document, a booklet of twenty-two pages, was approved by the hierarchy at their June meeting.[5] To appreciate its significance one ought to compare it with the former syllabus, an eleven page pamphlet, also published by Brown and Nolan and revised in 1953. The old syllabus has a stern ring to it, with the emphasis on the duty of religious instruction. In the prefatory note reference is made to the relevant canons in the Code on the serious obligation of parents. Religious instruction in secondary schools is important not only because the pupils are likely to hold an important place in the community, but also because, on account of their wider reading, they are 'more exposed to the subversive influences of the age'. Schools are warned that if they do not give a sound religious training 'they fail in the essential part of their work'. Teachers are reminded that theirs is a sacred duty. Superiors of schools have the duty to present all pupils for examination. Curiously enough, the verb 'should' occurs twenty-eight times in the four page preface. In this heavy atmosphere therefore of duty and obligation the few good counsels given to teachers are smothered. Even the basic aim offers little by way of challenge: 'The aim of the course is to produce good and enlightened Catholics, who will know and practise their religion, grasp its meaning in a vital manner, and appreciate its value for this life and the next.'

[4] December 1966.
[5] *Syllabus of Religious Instruction in Post-Primary Schools and Colleges*, Dublin, Browne and Nolan, 1966.

The 1966 syllabus represents 'a radical development', to quote from Cardinal Conway's brief preface. In the introduction a very positive note is sounded. The following are the key points:

1. The whole community, home and school, has the work of religious instruction.
2. The aim is to bring the student in contact with Christ. The teacher's role is to awaken and develop faith.
3. The core of our faith is the Easter Mystery, in which Christians are called to share.
4. This mystery of our dying and rising with Christ is unfolded in the history of God's dealings with man.

Teaching who Christ is means leading students to see that God is calling them—he is calling this class today—to a new life in Christ. In transmitting these truths the teacher, here referred to as catechist, draws upon four great sources—Bible, worship, doctrine and witness.

'This mystery proclaimed in scripture, celebrated in the Church's liturgy and formulated in her doctrinal teaching, is a call from God to which our pupils freely respond by prayer and Christian life.'

One difference that emerges from a comparison of the two programmes is a shift in emphasis from obligations, so evident in the 1953 revision, to values in the 1966 reform. A second difference is clearly discernible in the structure of the programme. Formerly there was a separation of the four sources mentioned above with separate examination questions in doctrine, liturgy, scripture, church history and, for the senior years, in social science as well. Now there is to be an integrated approach and church history will no longer be seen in isolation. The role of examinations, it would seem, is in abeyance. The third difference is found in the marked emphasis on discussion, especially for the senior years, with a list of optional topics being provided.

Arrangements of the subject matter for post-primary instruction—12-17 age group—is as follows:

1st Year, the story of our salvation; the creed.

2nd Year, Christ our life—the liturgy; grace and sacraments.

3rd Year, Response of our love; virtues and commandments.
4th Year, The Church of Christ; integrates church history.
5th Year, Jesus Christ our Saviour; witness in the world.

Public interest in the new syllabus has yet to manifest itself. On the other hand it cannot be said that the bishops have gone out of their way to bring it to the public's notice. Due to that odd mixture of modesty and pride which affects most Irish bishops in their dealings with the people of God, the faithful have not been made forcefully aware of this clear sign that their pastors are taking the Council's teachings seriously. Commitment to the change is not as wholehearted as one might expect. Enquiries among teachers reveal that in one diocese Sheehan's *Apologetics* must remain the chief text for senior classes. How relevant is this for a seventeen year old girl today? Another diocese will only implement the first year of the programme. Dublin appears to be watchful yet waiting; the former syllabus still holds. Presumably, the archdiocese will make its own adjustments since there has been a committee at work on the secondary school religion curriculum. If the results are anything like the new series of Dublin preliminary school texts now appearing then the outlook is hopeful.[6]

Two deficiencies are apparent from a study of the 1966 syllabus. In the first place, the majority of teachers lack the training necessary for its implementation. Efforts are being made in some dioceses to provide monthly lectures, but this is far too haphazard when one looks at the overall situation. Since the programme itself is 'a radical development', a more radical approach is called for to meet the needs of those who must give effect to it.

Secondly, there is no text available that adequately measures up to the needs of the course. Of the texts recommended (none is prescribed), four are American, one is in use in English schools and the other, not yet completed, is a translation from the French.[7] There is no attempt being made as yet to draw upon the resources of the whole Church in Ireland to publish suitable texts.

[6] *Word of Truth* series, Dublin Diocesan Primary Schools Commission. Book 1, *From God We Come*, text by Mary Purcell, Gill, Dublin, 1966.
[7] *Young Christians Today*, 5 vols., edited by Peter McConville, Chapman-Gill, 1966.

Even if this were realized in the coming year, it would be 1975 before a complete series of home-produced religion books would be available and in use. Perhaps this highlights the short-comings of any of the texts now recommended.

There could be no more tangible evidence of the breakdown in living transmission of the Christian message than this failure of the fifteen hundred year old Irish Church to produce adequate books for the instruction of the young in the Gospel. In a sense this means that the Gospel as a living local heritage of the Irish Catholic people has been lost, at least temporarily. The enlightened methods of modern catechetics and a scheme of contents which draws directly on the theology of Vatican II have been adopted in principle. But it has now become evident that this is not enough.

The urgent, really crucial task of relating the reformed methods and content to the specific life and history of a people, so that these can acquire sacred meaning and therefore meaning *tout court*, is equally imperative. With thousands of Irish missionaries abroad being pressed on all sides to relate the Gospel to the specific cultural contexts and histories into which it is being preached, it is odd indeed that this has not yet been done at home and that many trained catechists and appointed teachers of the people do not see the necessity of doing it.

Ironically, the imported 'up-to-date' texts recommended by the syllabus fail, whatever their other merits, to live up to two of the principal claims of the new catechetics : they fail to relate the Gospel to life and they fail to convey the Gospel to the young as the history of their salvation. Or rather, they are seriously inadequate, and necessarily so, in both respects. The only life to which the Christian message can really be related is life as known, experienced, and remembered by an historic community of people, and such life is always concrete, specific, and more or less locally rooted and conditioned. A 'history of salvation' which draws only, or almost exclusively, on the history of the Jewish people up to the first century AD is not the history of salvation of the Irish or the Germans or the Italians or of any other people now alive in the second half of the twentieth century. Imported texts cannot be adequate in either of these respects.

The Irish have a very ancient, continuous and clear-cut history of salvation. They are reputedly very conscious of their history and very attached to their local variant of life. They might therefore have been reasonably expected to pioneer the next step in the renewal of catechetics after the breakthrough in regard to general method and general content which was made on the European continent, and especially in Germany. Besides, since the history of their salvation in the eighteenth and nineteenth centuries is part of the history of salvation of each of the English-speaking churches, it would have been very useful indeed if they had done so.

In fact it seems that this next step in the catechetical renewal is already being taken in the Netherlands. A *New Catechism*, sub-titled 'Announcement of the Faith for Adults', and approved by the Dutch bishops, was published recently by Paul Brand, Hilversum. The first chapter 'Man the Questioner', which heads off the first section 'The Mystery of Existence', begins as follows :

'What questions were in the minds of the forefathers of the Dutch people when they accepted the faith ? These have been lost in the darkness of history.

'The spread of Christianity, which had got under way about 350 AD in South Limburg and the districts around Tongeren in Belgium, after the arrival of Servatius from Asia Minor, began considerably later in the North, when Willibrord landed on the Dutch coast about 690.'

This treatment of the early history of Dutch Christianity continues up to the middle of the second page. Only then is the first attempt made to relate the particular sacred history of the Dutch to the general aspects of the human condition mentioned in the section-heading and the chapter-heading.

Fortunately, the new Irish syllabus states clearly that adequate texts are not yet available to cover the new, reformed course. Fortunately too, it is widely accepted in Irish catechetical circles that the foreign texts at present in use or recommended are only a catechetical stopgap.

7

LOPSIDED AVANTGARDISM[1]

While it is true that the fiftieth anniversary celebrations through-out Ireland at Easter were not commemorating the establish-ment by international law of the free Irish state—that golden jubilee will occur in 1971—it seemed to most Irish people that this was the case. Even to the Protestant majority in Northern Ireland, whose public spokesmen had said that the celebrations were not such as could find sympathy with them, the Easter Rising of 1916 in Dublin represents in effect the birth of the Irish Re-public. The anniversary has been regarded in Ireland as a suitable occasion for assessing the achievements to date of the new state and the degree to which the various aspirations of the Irish revo-lution have been realized. Since the revolution and the state-building which followed it were almost exclusively the work of Catholics, the nature of the achievements and the measure of suc-cess are of concern to Catholics everywhere.

On Easter Monday 1916 in Dublin, a revolutionary junta of seven Catholics proclaimed a democratic republic with full re-ligious freedom. When these seven men and other leaders of the Rising had been executed, popular feeling moved massively be-hind their cause. An elected assembly empowered an executive to organize and prosecute warfare and to begin the civil adminis-tration of the country. With the support of labour strikes at home and diplomatic activity in the United States and Europe—there were even friendly contacts with the Bolsheviks—a national liberation movement took shape which set headlines for many anti-colonial revolutions in Asia, the Near East and Africa. Finally, a new state emerged which, despite civil war and other severe threats to civil stability, has maintained its democratic

[1] May 1966.

94

structure to the present day and inscribed the principles of the 1916 proclamation in its constitution. This state has been served by an impartial judiciary and by an incorruptible and efficient civil service and police force.

In the face of such facts a great deal of 'progressive' Catholic cant which has become fashionable in the last few years must pale somewhat, while at the same time betraying itself as a product of clerical mentality or of a ghetto so remote from contemporary history as to be impervious even to the newspapers. When confronted with the recent history of the Irish Catholic people—not to mention other easily ascertainable facts of life in English-speaking Catholicism—such phrases as 'dialogue with the world', 'religious liberty', 'activization of the laity', 'the end of the Constantinian era' [sic], 'common cause with other Christians', and 'facing up to modern realities' cannot maintain their pretensions as slogans of radical revolutionary novelty. If they are really to reflect some new, developing realities or some desirable but unrealized aspirations—if they are to be really meaningful—either their blanket application to the universal Church must cease or their formulation must be modified so as to express accurately something that is really novel everywhere. As they are at present used in English, such phrases often represent no more than a thoughtless parroting of continental European slogans which arose out of the specific historical circumstances of the Church in continental Europe.

For example, it simply does not make sense to speak of 'religious liberty' or 'separation of Church and state' as innovations in Catholic life and theory made possible by the Vatican Council when that very liberty has been included for decades past in the Irish constitution, with the approval of the Irish hierarchy, and when the Catholic Church in Ireland has never received even that mimimal financial support from an Irish Catholic government which the churches of Hungary, Rumania, Yugoslavia, or Eastern Germany receive from their Communist governments. When 'active participation of the laity in the Church' is understood solely in terms of action within the liturgical sphere or what has hitherto been the clerical sphere, then such activities as the building of a free and just civil society are excluded by implication from the domain of the Church's action and the devaluation of the lay role in the Church is reinforced by people who allegedly want to overcome it.

If the Protestant communities in the Irish Republic which were originally opposed to the new state have this Easter found their way to make qualified statements of loyal adhesion and to hold special religious services for the welfare of the nation, this has not been primarily because of recent courtesies among clerics or because of theological dialogue between priests and ministers. It has been primarily due to the fact that the Catholic political leaders of the new state regarded them as equal citizens, that the people elected a Protestant as their first president and that, in short, the new régime first surprised Protestants and then won them over by its sense of justice and its magnanimity. But, in view of the new ecumenical movement sanctioned by the Vatican Council, who could say that this purely civil, lay and untheological action of Irish Catholics was not an example of 'active lay participation in the Church'—though it was never called that?

The achievements of Irish Catholics in the sphere of democratic political practice during the past fifty years have been due, apart from native political talent, to the strong moral convictions of the people, the profound religious and political consensus, the heritage of Daniel O'Connell's pioneer work in organizing mass democracy, the nineteenth-century alliances with the English Liberals, the republican tradition inherited from certain Protestant patriots, and the relatively high degree of classlessness in the new society. The separation of the north-eastern part of Ireland from the new state has caused a great deal of anger and frustration over the years, both among those who were concerned about the disabilities of the Catholic minority in the North and among those who maintained the myth, despite all the evidence to the contrary, that the inhabitants of Ireland are one people and one nation. The degree of passion involved and the shibboleth quality of the myth have prevented the question being asked whether a substantial Northern Protestant bloc, hostile to democratic practice and riddled with religious bigotry, would really have been a valuable addition to the body of citizens—whether it would have helped rather than hindered the building of a stable democracy. Not only in regard to political and social ideals, but even where a sense of shared history is concerned, most Irish Catholics have more in common with tolerant, democratically-minded Englishmen than they have with the Ulster Protestants.

Just as the Irish in the nineteenth century played a key role in reconciling liberal democracy with Catholicism—an achievement that was to have profound results in North America and throughout the English-speaking world—a similar unideological assimilation of socialism began soon after the establishment of the free Irish state. When Pope John caused a flurry throughout the Catholic world from Italy to the United States by his approval and advocacy of 'socialization', a great variety of public state-sponsored enterprises were already an accepted part of the Irish economic structure. Since then, with the increasing industrialization and affluence of recent years, the principle that all the citizens must benefit materially and educationally from increases in the national wealth has been established as a public dogma and applied over-hastily in practice.

The talent of Irish Catholics for political and social aggiornamento—evidenced throughout English-speaking Catholicism, particularly in the United States, long before this Italian word became a slogan—can be seen in a broader Catholic context when it is contrasted with the one-sidedly theological aggiornamento of the German-speaking countries. If the last hundred years of Church history are seen as a whole, Irish-type and German-type Catholicism can be said to have provided two contrasting poles of Catholic modernism, not only in Northern Europe, but in the United States as well; from their respective centres on the East Coast and in the mid-West they have been the predominant influences in American Catholicism.

In an article in *New Blackfriars* in January 1966, 'How Progressive is German Catholicism?' Fr Charles Boxer, O.P., referred to 'the political activity of the Church in Germany' as 'the crisis area of aggiornamento' in that country. Fr Boxer's article, with its rather unbalanced selectiveness, its total lack of historical perspective, and its tendency to regard English political norms as an

D

absolute criterion, does less than justice to the positive achievements of German Catholicism in the political sphere. But the
author's main point holds good. The situation is cogently expressed by the German left-wing Catholic writer Carl Amery
(whom Fr Boxer quotes) :

> 'Nowadays we German Catholics are patting ourselves on the
> back because we have played such a progressive role in the
> Council. But, without taking away any credit from the Ger-
> man theological experts in Rome, our self-adulation is mis-
> placed. We Germans have a fatal talent for being satisfied with
> theoretical achievements while at the same time standing help-
> less before the burning practical, political and social ques-
> tions. . . .We must do something about this helplessness; we
> must build a bridge, or we will end up in a fatal theologizing,
> in what Karl Kraus has called "decorating your own home",
> hanging up the appropriate progressive diploma on the wall.'

Apart from the spheres of civil equity, social mobility, and the
socialization of resources, but interwoven with all of them, an
outstanding feature of Irish Catholic life in the past fifty years
has been a passionate devotion to the physical and material funda-
mentals of life, largely in isolation from spiritual or broadly
humanizing influences. Indeed in this respect there has been a
similarity to the mood in Russia since the revolution. Starting
from a much poorer industrial base, the actual achievements of
the Irish in terms of material standard of living put the much
trumpeted salvation through matter of the Bolshevik revolution
to shame; but the ugliness of the material productions in both
cases has been about equal.

How basic this zeal for the physical has been is illustrated by
two facts : the calorie intake from food in Ireland has for years
past been the highest in the world, and the Republic has a higher
density of hospital beds than any other country. The city of
Dublin can stand as an example. Famous for its slums fifty years
ago, it was recording the highest death rate of any European
city. In the 1920's the death rate was still 16·5 per thousand
residents; by the late 1950's it had fallen to an average of 10·3,

and there was less bad housing in Dublin than in London or Paris.

One of the reasons why the Irish live so much better today, materially, is that there has been a shortage of manpower in highly industrialized Britain and that the Irish revolutionary régime, unlike the Russian, did not prohibit emigration. Easy movement to Britain has materially benefited not only the emigrants but their families at home. As a study of the revolution reveals, the decision to permit emigration was not inevitable, and the fact that it was taken shows that the Irish political revolution, in contrast to the Russian and despite superficial appearances to the contrary, did not see a state power or a cultural dogma, but the material welfare and freedom of the people as its overriding aim.

Zeal for the crudely physical has been a predominant feature of Irish Catholic life since the second half of the nineteenth century. It has been accompanied by a divergent zeal for the purely spiritual which has produced a continual steep rise in ordinations and consecrations to the various forms of non-lay vocations; in ordinations to the priesthood, as in eating, Ireland leads the world. With the dramatic increase in wealth in recent years a new puritanism has developed which justifies everything from a theatre festival to a new park or the improvement of tablewear designs in terms not of enjoyment but of the economic gain to be hoped for. People have got used to reading this sort of thing in their newspapers:

'The sweetest music to come from the Seventh Waterford International Festival of Light Opera, which opened on Sunday, will be played on the cash registers of the city's shops, hotels, and guest houses.'

Some preachers, clerical and lay, admonish everyone to 'avoid materialism'. But like all purely negative exhortations, it has no hope of being heeded—especially when the predominant tendency of social and school education is towards crudely 'materialistic' goals.

Patrick Pearse, the most celebrated leader of the Rising, said: 'National independence must be understood to include spiritual and intellectual independence.' All the foremost revolutionary leaders down to Michael Collins were humanists who saw political freedom and economic betterment as the basis on which free personalities and freedom of mind could develop. The revolutionary programme has got bogged down in its basis. Split between divergent physical and spiritual zeals, lacking integrated vision and integrated language to express it, pursuing 'pragmatic' policies not merely because of an ingrained scepticism of ideologies but because of a sheer vacuum of ideas and inspiration, Irish Catholics have failed to develop a humanism which does credit to their faith and their revolution. As a consequence, they have had nothing of importance to say to their fellow English-speakers, to their fellow Europeans, or to their fellow Catholics. Intellectual activity has hardly risen above pedestrian commentary and positivist research conducted within narrow fields and insular horizons at several removes from life, first sources, and first questions. Life and works have been starved of imagination.

Unprejudiced observation of Catholic Ireland over the past few decades shows clearly that the image of the Irishman which the world has garnered from Irish literature and embroidered independently has a very lopsided relation to the reality. In the blurb to a collection of Frank O'Connor's short stories published recently in Germany this image is rendered as follows:

'Ireland, land of poets and dreamers, of the marriage-shy and the mamma's darlings, the pious and the superstitious, land of chaste maidens and clownish eccentrics.'

But the rather different character of real life in Ireland today is not new: it is a latter-day concentration of features which were already evident during the Irish Catholic expansion into the English-speaking world in the nineteenth century.

Administrators and politicians, soldiers and organizers of men, lawyers and policemen, builders (but not architects), healers (whether as pastors, doctors, or nurses), teachers and trainers (but not educators)—these have been the characteristic creative roles of the modern Irish Catholic, whether cleric or layman. With due allowance for modifications due to the indefinable 'Irish thing', the characteristic élite have been more like Romans than

Athenians, more Prussian than Latin, Soviet rather than Russian. Perhaps this is just another way of saying that they have been very typical specimens of 'modern man' in one of his most widespread and most dynamic variants.

The artistic and imaginative aridity of this cultural system and the mutual friction between it and many of the literary artists it has produced, both in Ireland and America, suggests another comparison : the modern Irish Catholic system has been a sort of Platonic republic in which public teachers, ordained and unordained, handed down a finished 'philosophy', while 'poets' —imaginers of all kind—were unwanted. The Easter Rising, insofar as its aims were cultural, was an effort to change this state of affairs. Perhaps the impulses from the Second Vatican Council will prove more effective.

8

FRUSTRATION AND ANTICLERICALISM[1]

For months past, apart from the 1916 Rising, 'frustration' has been the predominant theme of public discourse in the Irish Republic. Frustration is not a new phenomenon in Ireland. With the exception of the years 1917-21, it has been a marked feature of Irish Catholic life for over a century. On the one hand, the inordinately heavy emigration, on the other, tales told by modern Irish writers, have borne witness to it. In an age which has seen frustration accepted almost as a norm of civilization, people have often regarded the Irish as an extreme case; partly with good reason, partly because of a failure to take into account that your Irishman, whether Catholic or Ulster Protestant, has not learned as well as some others how to grin and bear it.

In view of this lack of stoic skill, it is not surprising that the persistent sense of frustration should erupt periodically and become particularly noticeable. The present wave of anger in the Republic is the latest instance of this. Disillionment with affluence on the part of some, the feeling of others that they have missed out in the share-out, would seem to be the immediate causes. For nearly a decade past, with a unanimity worthy of a totalitarian state, money-making has been preached as the universal panacea by government, opposition parties, state agencies, advertising men, and newspapers, while the Church, the schools, and the universities failed to provide any superior sense of purpose. Now that the money has been made, various minorities have vented the general disappointment in strikes and other bullying tactics that have held society up to ransom, in bombing incidents, and in anticlericalism.

[1] July 1966.

102

It is nothing new that people angry with themselves should seek a scapegoat in a powerful but unarmed minority. In the years preceding the last war in Europe, the Jews in Germany, the kulaks in Russia, and the clergy in Spain were made the butts of the widespread frustration then being experienced in each of those countries. Irrationally, the members of these minority groups were held collectively responsible for all existing ills, and a happy future was promised if only their influence or they themselves were eliminated.

There have been anticlericals in Ireland before, but they were men whom the clergy had opposed politically; they had concrete, personal grounds for their anger, which had thus a certain rational basis. What has now appeared among a certain minority goes beyond this : it is that sour, systematic and compulsive anti-clericalism which has left a trail of sneers and ugliness through modern European history. On the one hand, it is battening on the general malaise, on the other, offering an acceptable 'common front' line to anti-Catholic bigots. Its only beneficiaries (if its first victims can be called such) are those journalists and literati who would like to replace the clergy as the prime public moralizers, pontificators and general layers down of law. But the fact that doctrinaire anticlericalism in Ireland today rides the wave of a fever, and that fevers pass, gives ground for hope that this unpleasant thing, so foreign to the spirit of the conciliar movement, will not last.

Education, meaning primary and secondary schooling, has been a bone of contention in the Republic for some years past. It is clear that reform is needed, both in the methods and the content of teaching; on this all sections of opinion are agreed. However, since the primary schools are managed by clergymen and the secondary schooling is almost entirely in the hands of priests and religious—though the state prescribes the courses, inspects the teaching, and sets the examinations—attacks on the educational system are frequently turned into attacks on 'clerical control', the defects of the system being laid at the door of the clergy.

On 2 April last, these questions formed the central topic of discussion in a very popular television programme, 'The Late Late

Show'. Each week a panel of guest speakers is invited. The panel
on this occasion included Dr Conor Cruise O'Brien, the literary
critic and political commentator of United Nations fame, and
Brian Trevaskis, a university student and author of an anticlerical
historical play. Mr Trevaskis had been invited the previous week
as well. By calling the Bishop of Galway a 'moron', attacking the
building of churches in general and the new Galway cathedral in
particular (there were so many other useful things could be done
with the money), and by his wide-ranging remarks on the dire
influence of the clergy in education and other matters, he had
caused a furore that had expressed itself in hundreds of letters
to the newspapers, some for him, some against. In the programme
of 2 April he withdrew the word 'moron' and went on to express
his doubts as to whether the Bishop of Galway knew the meaning of the word 'Christianity'. The schools issue was raised, and
Dr O'Brien had a lot to say about the stranglehold which the
clerical managers, and 'ecclesiastical bureaucrats' generally,
exerted in the field of education.

In the second half of April Canon John McCarthy of Athlone
sent a letter to the newspapers in which he wrote:

'It has become popular in these days to invoke the Proclamation of 1916. The most frequently quoted passage—and one
that has found a voice or two even on the Late Late Show—
reads: "The Republic guarantees religious and civil liberty,
equal rights and equal opportunities to all its citizens . . .
cherishing all the children of the nation equally." Against this
declaration let us look coolly at the Late Late Show of recent
weeks. What do we see? A state-subsidized service used to give
repeated opportunities to paid contributors to proffer gratuitous
and slanderous insults to Irish citizens and to mock at traditional Irish values.

'We see the clerical school managers (who give a completely
unpaid service) arraigned in absentia and condemned unheard
by paid panellists who for the most part revealed an appalling
unawareness (I use no harsher word) of the duties, rights,
difficulties and frustrations of the managerial office. In all

this have we the equality of treatment of all citizens as envisaged in the Proclamation? Does one lose one's rights as a
citizen when one puts on a clerical collar or an episcopal
mitre? . . . When this is done on a state-subsidized service, is
it not a malfeasance of public moneys? . . . No one would wish
to curtail legitimate freedom of expression or informed
criticism . . . [but] is it that in this Jubilee Year, through
the wrong use of human freedom, a terrible ugliness is aborn-
ing?'

In *The Irish Times* of 25 April, the Canon was answered by
a faculty member of University College, Galway, Ian Linden.
Mr Linden wrote :

'Sincere congratulations on Canon McCarthy's ecclesiastical
doublethink. It seems strange that gentlemen who weekly hold
congregations in abject misery while they lambast them with
edicts on communism, strikes, pornography, even occasional
personal attacks, should be immune from identical treatment.
In a sense the weekly homily is a far graver insult to the Irish
Catholic citizen : it works on the assumption he is a moron and
or sex-maniac in most cases. . . . However, this must not blur
the fact that Telefis Eireann [Irish Television] is engaging in
un-Irish activities. I have long suspected communist infiltra-
tion : an investigation is imperative in the name of freedom.'

The Canon replied to Mr Linden regretting the latter's sneering tone and unsubstantiated generalizations. He pointed out that
he had not given a single sermon either on communism or
pornography for years, and that neither theme occurred in several
diocesan preaching programmes which he had consulted.

In an article in *The Irish Times* 1916 Supplement (7 April)
Conor Cruise O'Brien wrote with supercilious distaste of the role
played by the Catholic Church in Ireland since the Rising and
of the Catholic people's loyalty to their Church. In attacking once
more the clergy's influence on education, the kernel of his argument was a statistic from a recent official report on the schools.
This showed, he said, that of the children attending primary

schools in 1962-3, 54% had disappeared from the official records without trace and before taking their final examination. He then went on to quote Senator Owen Sheehy Skeffington, 'the most vocal and courageous critic of the system', on how scandalous this was.

Senator Skeffington is a sort of national institution, the country's great free-thinker of the Voltairean school, a man known for his forthright statements and speeches on everything he considers wrong and, more recently, for his lengthy post-humous rebukes to Pope Pius XII for his failure to intervene in politics and save the Jews. It so happened that Dr O'Brien had taken not merely his quotation, but his statistic as well, from a letter written by the Senator to *The Sunday Independent*. On 13 April, Fr D. Gallagher of Limerick, in a letter to *The Irish Times*, pointed out that the statistic quoted had been misread in the first place: the children it referred to made up not 54%, but roughly 1%, of the total primary school attendance in 1962-3. On 25 April, letters from Dr O'Brien and the Senator were published. While apologizing for their error, they maintained that the correction made no real difference to their basic contention.

In a country that has still to attain intellectual freedom, and where that freedom is sorely needed, the influence of doctrinaire anticlericalism on the public debate is unfortunate in the extreme. It imposes a straight-jacket on thought and encourages reflex—reactionary—thinking. A public pundit can 'consecrate' himself into more than episcopal authority simply by attacking 'clerical influences' loudly. The gullible can then be relied on to swallow what he says at least as uncritically as an illiterate peasant congregation accept what they hear from their parish priest. In such circumstances, free thought about what bishops say or do is barred. Educational reform is shelved in favour of anticlerical sniping and clerical defensiveness.

How restrictive of free comment these influences can be is best exemplified by *The Irish Times*. Protestant-owned and committed to a policy of free comment, it is also traditionally committed to casting a cold eye on Catholic bishops, except in those rare instances when a bishop happens to say something which fits in with the editorial line. Of late it has found itself increasingly compelled to sacrifice the former principle to the latter. This has occurred while the paper, under Douglas Gageby's editorship, continues to seek new Catholic readers by increasing its coverage of Catholic news; John Horgan's dispatches from Rome provided outstandingly good reporting on the final session of the Vatican Council. Its recent strenuous efforts to increase circulation in Belfast have probably exerted pressure in the other direction.

When the Archbishop of Dublin, in January 1965, ordered a crib of faceless figures to be removed from a church, *The Irish Times* found itself in the position of having to allege artistic merit for a crib which was considered artistically indefensible by Dublin's artist community. When last April Cardinal Conway of Armagh (in Northern Ireland) warned the Northern Ireland government that the Catholics intended to hold on to their schools, and would not consider integration, *The Irish Times* had to disapprove. It reported that the statement had caused 'dismay' in the North, though the fact was that most Northern Catholics found their own sentiments adequately reflected in the Cardinal's statement. Early this year, when the Bishop of Galway challenged the government policy of closing down one- and two-teacher schools, *The Irish Times,* predictable as ever, saw itself obliged to regard one- and two-teacher schools as indefensible. More, it scented battle and got quite excited. A 'Church-State clash on education' was trumpeted; the 'secularization' of schools was said to be in the offing. In fact, none of the Church's legal rights had been challenged, and the issue had to do merely with finance and with conflicting views on community welfare and pedagogy.

In short, anticlericalism tends to distract this ambitious newspaper from the high role it ascribed to newspapers in a recent leading article, namely, 'to help keep public life clear and healthy'.

When those big words from the history books, 'Church-State clash', 'secularization', and the like are bandied about today in Ireland—there has even been a debate on television on whether Faith hinders Progress—one can get the impression that children have got hold of a banal textbook of modern European history and are playing at a game called 'Let's Catch Up!' Meanwhile, abundant opportunities for adults to make new history are going unheeded.

It is hardly the time for Catholics, in Ireland or anywhere else, to try to resurrect the past or to perpetuate those features of the past which the Vatican Council has enabled them to overcome. Doctrinaire anticlericalism gives permanence to the division in the Church between clergy and laity and obstructs the emergence of the people of God. It makes the clergy draw together instead of opening out and merging, tempts bishops to make resentment into an excuse for lack of initiative, distracts the laity from the challenge to be the Church and to carry the Church, which has now been put to them squarely. Enemies of the Church can want these reactionary developments, but Catholics, if they are consistent, cannot. As for ecumenism, if it is accepted to mean outward sweetness and inward sourness, then it is not ecumenism at all.

In a word, since it is the frustration in Catholic life which causes Catholic anticlericalism, this frustration is the real enemy. The means of ending this frustration have now been given to the Church, but especially to the Church's pastors, by the Council. Such laymen as are intelligent enough to prefer happiness to gripe will seek out these means and make use of them; but the ultimate means of eradicating Catholic anticlericalism are now in the clergy's own hands.

9

DUBLIN'S ARCHBISHOP[1]

Writing under the pseudonym Michael Serafian, the author of *The Pilgrim*[2]—a book on the state of the Church seen from Rome during the Council—has hard words to say about the Roman Curia and its 'arbitrary' influence on Church government. 'Besides', he continues, 'this upsetting of the divinely appointed hierarchic order has involved analogous evils on the lower echelons of government.' The curial mentality infects some bishops in their government of their own dioceses. As examples, Serafian cites Cardinal Santos of the Philippines and Archbishop McQuaid of Dublin.

Of Archbishop McQuaid, Serafian writes that his 'curial' propensities had led him to forbid 'two Council theologians to speak in his diocese at the University and at theologates. The two theologians were Fathers John Courtney Murray, S.J., and Gregory Baum, O.S.A. Fr Baum was also invited to speak at the central seminary of Maynooth, but McQuaid wrote to the President to object to the invitation and to state that he, as the prime bearer of the care of souls in the suffragan territories, had forbidden this man to lecture. Fr Baum lectured there in spite of Archbishop McQuaid's strictures. During his reign, the Archbishop has kept up a running battle with Trinity College, Dublin, refusing to allow Catholics attending it to have a chaplain, forbidding Catholics under pain of mortal sin to attend it. Recently a Catholic, Frederick Boland—who gavelled Khrushchev during the famous shoe-incident in the United Nations General Assembly —was elected Chancellor of Trinity College. This fact, plus the new Catholic interest in ecumenism, has left Dr McQuaid's innate hatred of Protestants and his life-long drive against them somewhat at a loss. But in all these actions we discover the same

[1] July 1965.   [2] London, 1964.

109

high-minded attitude, the same substitution of juridical norms for
the one irreplaceable quality of a Christian—genuine charity.'

This is not the first time that Archbishop McQuaid has been
attacked. During his twenty-five years as archbishop he has become something of a myth, not least of all in his own archdiocese.
When John Horgan, writing in the English *Catholic Herald*
about the reception to mark the opening of the new diocesan
press office in April 1965, reported that the Archbishop moved
cheerfully among the guests, remarking that he was sure they
would be glad of a chance to 'see the ogre in his den', the
words quoted surprised only those who were not aware that Dr
McQuaid had a sense of humour.

The story of the 'banned Council theologians' has by this
time found its way around the world. Serafian's version is slightly
fuller, if not less hysterical and inaccurate, than one usually gets.
Mgr Tracy Ellis, the American historian, writing in *The Wiseman
Review* (London, Winter 1964-5) on 'The Irish in Relation to
Religious and Political Freedom', cites the banning of the two
theologians as his sole ground for the statement that there is a
grave lack of 'intellectual freedom' in the Irish Church as a whole.
A grave 'lack of fresh thinking' might have been a somewhat more
accurate description of the intellectual situation up until a few
years ago. There was never any difficulty about getting Fr
Courtney Murray's or Fr Baum's writings—and Dublin is not
Ireland, nor the Archbishop Dublin.

Besides speaking at Maynooth (as Serafian, but not Mgr
Tracy Ellis, mentions), Fr Baum was interviewed about the Council on television in Dublin, gave public lectures in Carlow, Cork
and Belfast, and spoke to seminary students in Milltown (Dublin) and Glenstal Abbey. Dr McQuaid did not write personally
or *per alium* to Maynooth about Fr Baum. Fr Courtney Murray
was indirectly discouraged from giving a projected lecture in
Dublin and did not come to Ireland at all.

Serafian's account of the situation with regard to Trinity College is misleading and partly inaccurate too. Trinity College was
founded in the sixteenth century as a Protestant university. For

centuries it allowed no Catholics to study there. On the hypothesis that it is still a 'Protestant' (i.e. Christian) university, Dr McQuaid has been charged with anti-Protestant and unecumenical attitudes because he has forbidden Catholics to attend it. But Canon F. R. Bourke of Killaloe, speaking at the (Anglican) Church of Ireland Synod in 1964, took a different view of Trinity College. Canon Bourke said: 'The trends of Trinity College at the present time are not favourable to our Church. Trinity College is becoming very largely a secular university' (*The Irish Times*, 14 May 1964). During the summer of the same year various Protestants, writing in the correspondence columns of *The Irish Times*, expressed similar concern.

The Archbishop has issued his prohibition annually in the course of the 'regulations' published at the beginning of Lent. Since 1937 it has been the custom in Dublin that these regulations should include not merely instructions about fasting and abstinence, but also warnings from the Archbishop about any other matters which in his opinion called for remark. In 1964, for instance, the regulations included admonitions against mixed marriages, obscene plays and evil literature, communism and careless driving. There was also a characteristic reminder—characteristic because of Dr McQuaid's known zeal for the corporal works of mercy—of the Christian duty to take loving care of old people.

Among the points always included has been a warning against attending Trinity College. In 1964 the Archbishop said:

'The Church forbids parents and guardians to send a child to any non-Catholic school, whether primary or secondary, or continuation or university. Deliberately to disobey this law is a mortal sin, and they who persist in disobedience are unworthy to receive the sacraments. . . . Nothing in the attitude or prescriptions of the Holy See concerning the very desirable movement of Christian unity has altered the very grave obligation of Catholic parents to preserve for their children, in every phase of education, our most precious heritage of the faith.'

In fact it has always been possible for any Catholic student who could put forward reasonably sufficient grounds to gain a dispensation from the Archbishop's prohibition. Besides, while it is unaccountably true that no Catholic chaplain has been provided within the College, a specially appointed curate of a central Dublin parish has been in charge of the spiritual welfare of Catholics attending Trinity.

As for the general charge of 'innate hatred of Protestants', no one in Dublin believes this of Dr McQuaid. Many Protestants have had experience of his personal kindness. In an interview given last December to *The Word* (a Catholic magazine), the Protestant Archbishop, Dr Simms, was asked about his relations with his Catholic colleague. Dr Simms said : 'I have met Archbishop McQuaid. He had been most kind to call on me when I came to Dublin and I returned the call. We've spoken to each other on many occasions.'

However, the annual reiteration of the Trinity ban, along with the rather gloomy tone of the 'regulations' as a whole, certainly contributed to the growth of Dr McQuaid's reputation as an 'ogre'. This lenten document, printed in heavy black, displayed in all church porches, and read carefully by the faithful, was the only substantial message from their Archbishop which really got through for years on end to the vast majority of Dublin Catholics. Dr McQuaid's pastoral letters (likewise normally in Lent) did little to offset the impression made. Masterly expositions of doctrinal themes, their language seemed to assume a devoted audience with earnest theological interests rather than the multifarious laity of a capital city, people involved in rapidly changing living conditions, exposed to most of the strong anti-Christian influences common to Western Europe today and, as heirs of a revolution, striving—the best of them at least—to make their city and country a better and freer place to live in; people renowned moreover for their love of living language. Added to this was the fact that Dr McQuaid, a retiring and shy man, was not to be seen 'around town'. He has not made use of television or of sound radio; and there is no diocesan newspaper.

Ignorance is the breeding ground of myth, and ignorance of Dr McQuaid certainly played a part in developing the 'ogre' myth. There were also, however, the public facts already men-

tioned. Around these and around other facts Dr McQuaid's
image was constructed—fairly and unfairly.

Some discreet telephone calls over the years from Archbishop's
House to Dublin newspaper offices led, when news of the calls
had spread, to a belief among inexperienced people that the
Archbishop exercised a sort of secret control over what was
printed and broadcast in Dublin. Those who worked on newspapers, in radio, or television, knew that the Archbishop was only
occasionally a factor to be reckoned with; as in every capital city
most of the 'pressures' and 'bans' came not from Church circles
but from Government circles, business interests and other groups,
from newspaper editors, literary editors, and programme directors. In matters concerning the Church the norm in Dublin
journalism has rather been self-censorship arising out of uncertainty in the religious terrain on the part of Catholic journalists.
(Only one newspaper, *The Evening Press*, has overcome this complex.) Cases have indeed occurred of Dublin editors submitting
articles and news items to diocesan officials for prior approval
only to be told that a decision did not fall within the competence
of the diocesan administration.

Foreign journalists visiting Dublin on behalf of international
newspapers and magazines, their normal good sense inhibited by
the necessity of finding 'Irish' colour and by their unease in face
of a 'Catholic country', were sure to include something about the
all-pervasive influence of 'the Archbishop' (sometimes the plural
was used) in their dispatches. What they wrote was read in Ireland. On the other hand, an Irishman, Peter Lennon, writing
last year in the English *Guardian*, made his break-through in
journalism by devoting an entire article—one of four on the evils
of Ireland—to Dublin's 'Grey Eminence'. This article, much discussed in Dublin, was regarded as having 'broken the taboo of
silence'. But no great noise ensued—at least not in regard to the
Archbishop. As before, an occasional anonymous attack appeared
in the daily press; as before, these attacks merely displayed the
pique of individuals who were jealous of bishops in general and
who saw in Dr McQuaid's reputation an ideological opportunity.

The parish clergy of the archdiocese have been a special object
of Dr McQuaid's pastoral zeal. He has done much to ensure that

they maintain high moral and spiritual standards and cause no scandal to the laity. It is *their* freedom of expression and of action, rather than that of the laity, that has suffered under the archiepiscopal discipline. Personal initiative has often been hamstrung. Men engaged in adventurous biblical studies have been obliged to lie low. The faculty of philosophy in University College, Dublin—predominantly manned and attended by clerics—is susceptible to the Archbishop's influence. Its dull record has not helped to distinguish a university that is, in certain other aspects, intellectually alive. Understandably then, many people were surprised when, on the inauguration of an Irish television service several years ago, it transpired that Dr McQuaid had some time previously sent a group of his priests to America for training in television. This group has since produced some of the most distinguished and professional documentary films seen on Telefís Éireann.

The architecture of several large new Dublin churches came in for a great deal of criticism. They were pastiches of ancient styles, with a leaning towards the Byzantine. Never in fact in fifteen hundred years had Irish church architecture sunk so low. It was said in one or two cases that the Archbishop had rejected better designs in 'modern' styles. Meanwhile, in dioceses remote from Dublin, churches were being built in new styles, some of them excellent. Stories went the rounds of visits by the Archbishop to new religious buildings, in the course of which he was said to have ordered some piece of sculpture or devotional art in 'modern' style to be removed. The Archbishop never joined in the widespread criticism of the new Dublin churches nor did he condemn 'repository art'; some would have expected him, as bishop, to lead the criticism. No one could have guessed that Dr McQuaid, earlier in life, had acquired an excellent and sympathetic knowedge of modern French painting.

Some years ago a Dublin theatre festival, already planned, fell through when the Archbishop made known that he would not celebrate a Votive Mass to marks its opening, as at first he had agreed. It was intimated by the archdiocesan office that Dr McQuaid did not view kindly a play by O'Casey and a play based on Joyce which were being performed. The festival committee decided to abandon the festival. As one Dublin Protestant remarked at the time :

'Irish Catholics are full of brave talk and the most liberal sentiments about religion when you talk to them as individuals. But let them form a committee and run into some difficulty with the Church authorities, and they collapse like a pack of cards.'

Certainly there are some Catholics in Dublin who find in Dr McQuaid's reputation an excuse for facile bravery. In such circles the myth has it that 'you will lose your job' if you disagree openly with him. The 'job'—an excuse for timidity which Patrick Pearse noted in Dubliners long before there was an Archbishop McQuaid —is the reason given by these people for not saying the brave things which they would, of course, say if things were otherwise.

The word 'legalistic' has been used to describe some of the Archbishop's behaviour; for instance, in regard to his concern for strict Church control of new educational ventures where non-Catholics were also involved. It was even believed that Dr McQuaid's concern for his canonical rights had involved him in some dispute about the height of his throne relative to that of the Archbishop of Armagh during the annual bishops' conference in Maynooth. (The Archbishop of Dublin is, historically, Primate of Ireland; the Archbishop of Armagh Primate of All Ireland.)

Serafian says 'a lack of charity'. The poor of Dublin would not agree. The thousands who receive free meals from the diocesan funds, the strikers' families whom the Archbishop has helped, the tinkers' children who go to school in a bus paid for by him, and many others, probably see in Dr McQuaid their loving father in Christ. These, and many others who are not materially poor, are those 'good ordinary people' (the Archbishop's own words) whom he seems to regard as his special flock.

With the 'good extraordinary' people—not to speak of the 'ordinary bad'—the situation is somewhat different. A number of priests and laymen who have had occasion to write to the Archbishop seeking his approval for some enterprise, have received letters in reply which seemed unnecessarily sardonic—and some of these letters have been shown around and talked about. Those extraordinary people who need and would welcome the 'spiritual bread' of inspiring and encouraging words from their bishop have often been disappointed, some to the point of growing bitter. Especially during the past seven years, when Dublin has been the centre of an economic and mental revolution almost equal in scope to the earlier political revolution—and when this transformation was soon accompanied by the excitement emanating from the Council and the aggiornamento movement generally—such people have felt the lack of guidance and leadership—of 'notice' —from their bishop. Moreover, living in a state in which the civil authority has often used its funds to establish public enterprise where private initiative lacked the necessary resources, some Dublin Catholics have wondered why the Church authorities have not done the same, making good music and hymns in the churches, a permanent exhibition of good devotional art, a bureau for church design, courses in theology and the Bible as easily available throughout the archdiocese as are the other forms of knowledge.

The Archbishop's relationship to public affairs in the broadest sense also comes under the heading of 'charity', especially since his archdiocese includes the capital city. Practising Catholics predominate in the state leadership. The state is well disposed towards the Church; its leaders have openly professed adherence to the social teachings of Pope John. The Church benefits from all of this. Yet no one knows whether the Archbishop of Dublin appreciates a loyalty and devotion to Christian principles unusual in governments today. Dr McQuaid's only known judgement of the state's actions was a negative one. When, in 1951, the Irish bishops condemned a proposed public health service (since introduced in a modified form), Archbishop McQuaid's correspondence with the then Minister of Health was published in the newspapers.

It has been said that Dr McQuaid has a special admiration for Cardinal Cullen, that great nineteenth-century churchman formed by thirty years of life and high office in Rome who, as papal legate and Archbishop of Dublin, 'romanized' the Irish

Church and, in a sense, gave definitive shape to modern Irish Catholicism, especially to the episcopal part of it. He was also a man whom few knew well, a centre of controversy. One of his opponents, John O'Leary, a Fenian revolutionary, described him as

'one of the most dogmatic, domineering, and self-willed of men, with much of what he took to be, and what in a sense was, religion, but with apparently no feeling for his country other than that it was a good Catholic machine, fashioned mainly to spread the faith over the world'.

It is perhaps not merely a coincidence that, until recently at least, a good number of Dr McQuaid's Dublin critics could have made a very similar comment about their present archbishop, the main difference being that instead of 'for his country' they would have said 'for life'.

The Council came and with it the journalistic division of the 2,500 infinitely varied and nuanced individuals who govern the Roman Church into 'conservatives' and 'progressives'. Dubliners realized that they had a 'conservative' archbishop. A general movement of open criticism within the Irish Church had got under way a few years previously: priests and laymen were criticizing the clergy. This movement now acquired an ideological wing. As well as criticism, public sneering and angry attacks were heard, so that Dr McQuaid was soon not the only one in Dublin of whom Serafian might have said that he lacked 'the one irreplaceable quality of a Christian'.

Dr McQuaid did not tell his people that the aggiornamento was a good thing or a bad thing. He did not encourage—to put it mildly—visits of foreign 'progressive' theologians to his diocese. He simply began to carry out the new ordinances and counsels from Rome as loyally as he had the old ones. Some 'progressive' Dublin Catholics, who were previously in a quandary about whether to support the orthodox 'progressive' line on more authority for the local bishop, may have begun to wonder whether strict loyalty to Rome is such a bad thing, when 'Rome' becomes not the Curia but the Council. Dr McQuaid has, however, gone further. Several recent signs have shown that he understands the pastoral disadvantages of his 'ogre image', and not merely the letter, but the spirit, of the conciliar aggiornamento.

At the beginning of January last, Dr McQuaid ordered the removal of the crib from the new church at Dublin Airport. It was an unconventional crib, to say the least; its figures had been carved by a Dublin artist best known for his humorous wooden souvenir figures. To the surprise of many, some discussion in the press occasioned an explanatory statement from the Archbishop's office. The figures in the crib were 'beneath the level of human dignity in that they are not human'. Besides, it was 'an offence against Canon Law and the prescriptions of the Holy See to propose for public veneration figures purporting to be sacred without the previous sanction of the Archbishop'. As it so happened, in this particular case the Archbishop's opposition to experiments in devotional art was entirely justifiable. Some people did say that he should have waited until the Christmas season was over and then have intimated quietly that the crib should not reappear. But this sounded strange in view of the fact that for years previously Dr McQuaid had been reproved for his 'secretive' and 'hidden' way of doing things.

This year (1965) the lenten regulations contained no reference to Trinity College. For the first time since the nineteen-thirties they were confined to the questions of fasting, abstinence, and the fulfilment of Easter duties.

Dr McQuaid has also departed from his previous practice by permitting priests to lecture within the walls of Trinity College. An Anglican member of the College staff, Rev. E. C. T. Perdue, who was making arrangements for the observance of Church Unity Octave, asked the Archbishop to allow a priest to lecture on the Second Vatican Council. Dr McQuaid agreed, and is understood to have personally nominated the lecturer, Dr P. F. Cremin. Dr Cremin is Professor of Theology and Canon Law at St Patrick's College, Maynooth. Subsequently, Dr Enda McDonagh, another Maynooth professor, spoke in Trinity.

In the past two years Dr McQuaid has taken what for him is a new line by asking Catholics to join in the prayers during

Church Unity Octave. The form of words he used, in inviting prayers, was 'that Christians separated in doctrine and discipline from the Catholic Church may, by the Mercy of God, rejoin the One True Church of Christ'.

A change in another area, announced on 13 March last, was the establishment of a press relations office for the archdiocese— one of the few such offices in the world. The announcement explained that this was 'in accord with the decree on the media of social communication approved and promulgated by the Second Vatican Council'. The first head of the office is a layman, an experienced Dublin journalist, Mr Osmond Dowling.

Perhaps this press office and the fact that it was set up so soon after the decree are the best symbols of Dr McQuaid's own aggiornamento. It is not likely, however, that the extraordinary people of Dublin will be satisfied with half-measures. They will probably continue to feel the need of a bishop who obviously shares their concerns and who gives them clear leadership in their desire to make those concerns serve earthly Christian purposes. But they can now afford to be more hopeful. And there is also more hope that the ordinarily bad people of Dublin will hear saving words in time.

However, the publication in Studies *(Winter 1965) of 'The Church in Dublin: 1940-1965. A study of the Episcopate of Most Reverend Charles McQuaid DD', by the editor, Roland Burke Savage, S.J., occasioned the following disappointed comment in* Herder Correspondence, *April 1966:*

An article in *Herder Correspondence*, July 1965, dealt with Dr McQuaid, Archbishop of Dublin. It was the first time that the accumulated criticism surrounding both Dr McQuaid's policies and his person as bishop were faced up to publicly, unpolemically, and with the simple intention of establishing the truth. That the situation we described remains substantially unchanged has been evidenced by the general course of events and not least by the above-mentioned apologia for Dr McQuaid on the occasion of his silver jubilee as bishop. The main title of the forty page essay is misleading, since the essay deals only with those aspects of Catholic life and achievement in Dublin which interest the Archbishop and with those kinds of Catholics who effectively

claim his attentions. Just praise is given to the excellent adminis-
trator, the builder of churches and schools, the helper of the
physically sick and handicapped, the organizer of almsgiving to
the poor—outstanding merits which no one disputes. But we are
also reminded once more of those other traits—the unconquered
shyness, the martyr complex, the dislike of public occasions, the
penchant for the unnecessarily harsh or humiliating phrase—
which have done so much to give an impression of negativeness,
to spread discouragement and sourness, and to foster disrespect,
resentment, and cynicism among Dublin Catholics of all ages.
That Dr McQuaid can console the sick and dying no one doubts;
that he can inspire the quick and healthy, open vistas for live
wires, no one has experienced—and the crux of the matter lies
here. Fr Burke Savage ignores this. Nothing stranger than his
scathing rebuke to Irish Catholics as a body for regarding the
public persona of a bishop—and not merely his 'policies'—as a
proper subject for comment and, if necessary, complaint. A
bishop reduced to 'policies' is no successor to the apostles, no
colleague of John XXIII. That Dr McQuaid's personal one-
sidedness has produced a pastoral situation which calls urgently
for repair is clear to anyone who listens to Dubliners. Every public
man has his unfortunate incidents, and Dr McQuaid's share, by
now so ridiculously magnified, would have been forgotten long
ago if his language were different and if he came across as an
inspiring guide of men. Certainly he has his malicious detractors,
but they merely exploit a situation—they did not create it. One
of the stated aims of this well-informed and charmingly written
jubilee essay is to show how Dr McQuaid 'has inspired the clergy
. . . and the faithful of the Archdiocese to give of their best'. But
this is not shown and could not be shown, for Dr McQuaid has
simply not done this: all those priests and laity who say he has
done otherwise cannot be wrong. Fr Burke Savage's apologia
does not affect the heart of the matter for no apologia could do
that. Perhaps it should not matter quite so much to Christians
what their bishop is like; but one of the boomerang effects of a
century and more of clergy identifying the Church with themselves alone is that it matters very much what the bishop is like
—it matters inordinately.

10

THE MYTH OF THE IRISH:
A FAILURE OF AMERICAN
CATHOLIC SCHOLARSHIP[1]

For slightly more than a decade American Catholics have been
engaging in or listening to an intensive public discussion about
certain defects of Catholic life and thinking in the USA. The
dissatisfactions have been grouped under four main headings:
authoritarianism, obsessive hostility to sexuality, ghetto mentality,
and anti-intellectualism or non-intellectualism. (These last two
words have been used to cover such a variety of complaints that,
ironically, they have caused much mental disarray. Basically this
has happened because 'intellectualism' has often been taken to
mean 'right' i.e. 'liberal' attitudes and opinions or even the
'right' kind of passion and emotion.)

A substantial part of the discussion has dealt not with the
phenomenology of these defects, but with their historical genesis.
Logically this should have led to a fresh examination of the
history of the Roman Catholic Church over the past century
and a half and to critical studies of the European and Anglo-
Saxon cultures from which the Church has largely drawn its
cultural substance. The defects identified by American Catholics
were common to late Tridentine Catholicism as a whole. They
have been inveighed against for years past by theological and
other writers on the European continent, identified in countries as
different from each other as Germany and Spain. However,
although many of these critical writings have been available in
translation in the United States, the historical discussion of
American Catholic defects has not followed this logical course
to any important extent. There were several reasons for this.

[1] November 1966.

The mass of American Catholics thought of their church as something quite special and apart within Catholicism. Consequently, any explanation of its characteristics or defects tended to be special too. Partly because of their history as immigrants, but also due to Anglo-Saxon cultural influences, American Catholics regarded nationality or race as the over-riding and autonomous determinant of culture and people. They saw nationality as a force fixing the mould of people's lives quite independently of broader cultural influences or historical change. (The English have long held the same view; the Irish, in an extreme form at least, since the nineteenth century.) Besides, for over a century it had seemed to the mass of Americans, whether Catholics or not, that there was some intrinsic connection between Catholicism and Irish nationality. Supporting this impression was the obvious and well-known fact that nineteenth-century Irish Catholics had played a decisive role in shaping the Church in America. The Irish were indeed the founding fathers of American Catholicism as it exists today.

For these reasons, the historical discussion of the four deadly sins of American Catholicism veered narrowly towards Irish Catholic history; and American Catholic scholarship offered no effective resistance, opened no wider historical vistas. Since, as a matter of fact, nineteenth-century Irish Catholicism offers nothing of definitive importance to the researcher into the origins of Catholic authoritarianism, sexual puritanism, ghetto mentality, or intellectual sterility, this was an unfortunate detour to begin with.

In theology and ecclesiastical practice Irish Catholics were zealously orthodox—'terribly orthodox' we would be inclined to say today. In these spheres the word of Rome was law, and a zealous romanizing movement transformed the people's religion. *The Irish Ecclesiastical Record*, founded in 1854 as the first theological journal for Catholic priests to be published in English, made a significant choice of motto from the dictum of St Patrick : *Ut Christiani ita ut Romani sitis.* Neither in Rome, during a period when the Curia was quick to pounce on deviations, nor in the Catholic countries of Europe, were Irish Catholics held to be remarkable for any of the four deadly sins which occupy the centre of the present American debate. The documents show this.

In many ways the century was the most provincial—the least 'Irish'—in Irish history. It saw the definitive loss or abandonment of the Irish language and of the traditional Irish religion and culture. In the resulting vacuum, both culture and religion were derived to an extreme degree from the English-speaking and Protestant environment on the one hand, and contemporary European Catholicism on the other. In the sense that America experienced the ancient cultural-religious syntheses of French, German, and Italian Catholicism, it never experienced Irish Catholicism.

Indeed the only profitable harvest of self-understanding which American Catholics might stand to gain by occupying themselves with Irish Catholicism would be in respect of those features of Irish Catholic life which were noted as exceptional on the Continent generally or which caused disquiet in Rome : the closeness of clergy and people, Irish views on Church-state relations, beliefs and practices in regard to liberal democracy, revolutionary tendencies and activities in the fields of state politics and land ownership. As it happens, however, American Catholics are not urgently concerned about these aspects of their heritage.

Still more unfortunate than this detour in itself was the failure of American Catholic scholarship to follow it through by a sound investigation of religion and culture in Ireland during those decisive decades of the nineteenth century. The academic apparatus was ready to hand : American Catholics maintain over three hundred institutions at university and college level. However, to judge by the writings published over the past decade, this necessary investigation has not been made. Moreover, the writings of American scholars during these years, insofar as they have touched at all on Irish Catholic life and history in the nineteenth century, have shown little evidence of an appreciable acquaintance with the rapidly growing body of relevant work being produced by Irish historians and by some of their English colleagues. (No other century of Irish history has been receiving such concentrated attention on the European side of the Atlantic.)

As a result, when the historical discussion of American Catholic defects veered towards Ireland, it did so in an atmosphere of ignorance and produced a scapegoat myth. The detour became a blind alley.

While some were still asking tentative, unanswered questions about the Irish contribution (cf. Thomas F. O'Dea in *The American Catholic Dilemma*, p. 122),[2] others supplied firm conclusions : the origins of the American Catholic evils were to be found in Irishness. Since knowledge and understanding of nineteenth-century Ireland were lacking, and since the origins sought for lay elsewhere, these origins were not in fact discovered in the nineteenth-century Irish Catholics. They were discovered in 'the Irish' understood as a timeless entity, a tribe abstracted from the United Kingdom, the British Isles, the Church of Rome, modern Europe, humanity, and history, and therefore easily assumed to include those very real, live Irish Catholics, immersed in particular historical circumstances, who emigrated to America in the nineteenth century.

Basically it was the stock Irish of American and Irish-American legend who were thus warmed up and put to new uses, a people, as eternal and as adaptable to myth as the Jews, who were thus brought to the rescue of the American Catholic malaise and of American Catholic liberal respectability. What had once been a proudly claimed racial heritage, which offered some relative practical advantages and which had therefore frequently been claimed by people who had no strict right to it, was now pilloried and disowned for the sake of greater advantages—for a feeling of purity and moral superiority and for the glittering chance of belonging more completely to the central American establishment. To a lesser extent, as in some cases where the evils of Irishness were rubbed in by bearers of German and Slav names, it was a paying back of old ethnic scores, a rebellion of the 'subject peoples' of American Catholicism against that Irish hegemony which in times gone by had been intolerant of their national separatisms and all too eager to americanize them.

Certain journalists and publicists, who sought association with American liberals rather more than with their fellow Catholics, began to fill the vacuum of real knowledge in regard to the nineteenth-century Irish which had been left by the scholars. They

[2] Sheed and Ward, New York, 1958.

filled it with myth, the general import of which was that the
trouble with American Catholicism was that it was Irish rather
than Catholic, that Irish cultural and even racial characteristics
had distorted Roman Catholicism in Ireland before it ever
reached America, and that the Irish had imbued first their own,
and then American Catholicism, with precisely those characteristics which every enlightened American must find hateful. 'I
would go so far as to suggest', opined John P. Roche in *The Reporter* (26 March 1964),

> 'that theology is irrelevant—that the anti-intellectualism, the
> puritanism, the social dogmatism that has been so characteristic
> of the Church in America is a consequence of its Irishness, not
> of its Catholicism.'

In his fourteen thousand word survey of American Catholicism
in *The Saturday Evening Post* (28 November 1964), R. F.
Sheehan quoted the Protestant theologian Reinhold Niebuhr as
saying to him that the reason why the American church had failed
to measure up to the challenges of the modern world was that it
was 'an Irish church'. This as a prelude to a disquisition by the
author on 'Irish Jansenism'.

All the stock marks of racialist propaganda were there, from
the charge of pathological sexuality down to Sheehan's reference in his *Post* article to the 'Maynooth odour', which was in dire
contrast to the 'fragrance of good Pope John'. One of the nastiest
thrusts came from Michael Novak in *New Republic* (22 August
1964). He was discussing the coming election and the factor of
'white backlash' or anti-negro feeling which might affect the
Catholic voter. There were three factors that made the American
Catholic indifferent to the justice of the negro's claim. The third
of these was the strict sexual morality which made Catholics
susceptible to the whispers of immorality of the negro ghetto-
dweller.

> 'Fear and envy [sexual, presumably] are compounded; the
> special brutality of Irish policemen may have its sources here.'

(See also an address by Novak printed in *The National Catholic
Reporter*, 30 March 1966.) Significantly, those Catholics who

most vehemently decry anti-negro and antisemitic prejudice prove the most prone to systematic anti-Irishism—one of the few racial dislikes still permitted to American liberals.

At the same time, the insinuation or direct allegation of heresy lent Torquemadan overtones to the myth-making. 'Irish Jansenism' became a household word among Catholic intellectuals, though there is no reference to it in the records of the Roman Curia. Michael Novak, who has made himself quite a specialist on Irish depravity, referred to authoritarianism as the 'Celtic heresy' in *Commentary* (September 1965), quite a serious magazine.

As the ardour of the myth-makers rose, the myth assumed an ultimate form. It was given out as an unmitigated misfortune for the American Church that the Irish had been the preponderant ethnic group in American Catholicism rather than, say, the French or the Germans. This contention was buttressed by references to the achievements of French and German Catholics in Europe (not in Canada or the United States) in the twentieth century. Believing in this judgment of the Irish contribution meant ignoring a great deal that was obvious, but first and foremost the good fortunes of the American Catholic community and of the American church under 'Irish' leadership. It meant ignoring that the United States are an English-speaking country, that the Irish were the only Catholic immigrants who spoke English, that they shut themselves off from native American life much less than any of the other Catholic groups, and that they took to American politics like fish to water—a characteristic that was to have far-reaching consequences. Further, it meant attributing no positive significance to a fact recorded by John D. Donovan in *The Academic Man in the American College*,[3] namely, that more Catholic university professors have come from an Irish-American milieu than from any other ethnic background. Yet so great, apparently, was the need to believe, that belief proved possible. Or perhaps this ultimate form of the myth was that ultimate outrage to reason and empirical knowledge which often induces the credulous to accept something on faith. One way or another, intellectualism had found strange advocates

[3] New York, 1964.

As every communist party and totalitarian government knows well, myth can flourish only when information about the subject is not readily available. Since this American Catholic myth is basically about Irish Catholicism understood as a function of a fixed quantity—'the Irish' or 'Irishness'—information even about contemporary Irish Catholicism could have seriously undermined its credibility. The myth has in fact been buttressed by the paucity of information on contemporary Irish Catholicism in the American magazines. Although *America* and *Commonweal*, to cite two obvious examples, have correspondents in Europe, and though their range covers the world, one will search in vain for reports on recent cultural and religious developments in Ireland. Since it would be a considerable understatement to say that American Catholic interest in things Irish would warrant such reports, their absence is, to say the least, remarkable.

Here then was a really decisive challenge to American Catholic scholarship. The Irish scapegoat myth was being widely propagated. It was being accepted by the mass of young college-educated Catholics as readily as the communist myth was accepted in Senator McCarthy's days by that mass of un-enlightened Catholics whom the new breed of graduates affect to despise—as passively as the antisemitic myth was accepted in Germany in the thirties. Yet the scholars, the historians in particular, did not get down to work. Professor O'Dea's tentative questions (he asked them in 1958) have remained un-answered by himself and by documentary evidence on nineteenth-century Ireland. The scholars have not protested, nor made a plea for right reason, nor called for documentation, research and proofs. On the contrary, some of them have lent their voices to the strengthening of the myth, the latest examples being Fr Joseph F. Scheuer and Edward Wakin in their joint work *The De-Romanization of the American Catholic Church*.[4]

Only in May of this year, when this new foray of Catholic anti-intellectualism had been running its course for nearly a decade, did Professor Philip Gleason of Notre Dame University, writing in *America* (14 May), call for respectful scrutiny of the historical facts. The magazine presented his article thus: 'A pro-

[4] New York and London, 1966.

fessor of history takes up the cudgels in defence of the Irish contribution to the Church in America.' This, and Professor Gleason's uncontradicted reference at the beginning of his article to the 'critical barrage' of anti-Irishism during recent years, provide succinct documentation on the state of the question.

Later, in a review of *The De-Romanization of the American Catholic Church* in *Ave Maria* (10 September), Professor Gleason had this to say :

'When other forms of historical inventiveness fail, Wakin and Scheuer can be depended on to make some derogatory allusion to the Irish. . . . Since the Irish did play so important a role in the American church, it is all the more regrettable that Wakin and Scheuer have chosen to abet the anti-Irishism that seems to be becoming the antisemitism of liberal American Catholics, rather than trying to discuss the matter in a halfway intelligent fashion. But in view of the paucity of their research, they are hardly equipped to discuss it at all. . . . Despite the meagreness of their research, Wakin and Scheuer pretend to know all there is to know about Irish Catholicism.'

Professor Gleason went on to point out that Wakin and Scheuer had failed completely to relate what they say of Irish Jansenism in regard to sex to de Tocqueville's comments, during a journey in Ireland in 1835, on the freedom from prudery of the Irish as compared with the French; nor what they write on Irish hostility towards marriage to the inordinately high Irish marriage rate in the first half of the nineteenth century. Professor Gleason then continued :

'And while we are on the subject, where is all this research on the mother-complex of the Irish Americans? Impressionistic evidence indicates that there is something to it, but what are the studies that allow Wakin and Scheuer to generalize so freely on the mother mystique that the Irish "contributed" to American Catholicism?'

These defects, and others noted earlier in his review, led Professor Gleason to comment :

'It remains only to add that the authors of this wretched book dare to lecture us on the nature of true intellectualism. It is to laugh.

'But on second thought, it is more an occasion for tears and lamentation than for laughter. For this is not a prank of school-boys. These two men are faculty members of one of the lead-ing American Catholic universities; a member of the editorial board of *Cross Currents* apparently acted as midwife in the delivery of their scholarly labours; parts of it have appeared before publication in quite respectable journals. . . .

'This book is infinitely worse than none at all. It is worse than none at all because all the issues that Wakin and Scheuer have mauled in so oafish a fashion really do exist; and they are problems of the most serious sort for American Catholicism.'

The success of the Irish scapegoat myth and the failure of scholarship to forestall it or effectively to refute it point to some-thing more than that 'lack of industry and the habits of work' with which Mgr Tracy Ellis charged Catholic academics in his celebrated discourse ('American Catholics and the Intellectual Life') in 1955.

The discussion about the historical genesis of Catholic ills has been carried on by the theorizing and literary element of the Catholic community. This composite category included, as well as scholars whose primary aim is demonstrable truth, other men—journalists, publicists, scholars—whose primary aim is to produce certain effects by means of words—effects serviceable to their own needs and to the needs of others like them. The desire for an historical understanding of American Catholic ills has not been the only motivation at work in the discussion. Other, con-flicting motivations have inhibited and deflected the search for understanding, nourished the Irish myth, and inhibited reaction against it.

American Catholics, in their total relationship to life, suffered from that all-too-human split in the soul which Christianity is meant to heal, but which late Tridentine Catholicism failed to heal. Many, projecting their internal malaise in terms of their environment, saw their trouble as somehow connected with their

E

split relationship to American life. As the numbers of college-educated Catholics grew, so too did the number of theorizing and literary types who saw this alienation from the mainstream of American life as occurring essentially in the realm of ideas and language.

Professor O'Dea, in the book already referred to, puts this problem clearly :

> 'On the one hand we have formed a firm identification with certain aspects of the national culture—notably in the fields of politics, constitutional law, and economics. On the other, we have developed in certain areas an aloofness amounting at times to alienation. This is especially true with respect to the development of native thought in spheres involving basic world views and values, where our past has made homogeneity with the Protestant derived tradition difficult or even impossible.
>
> '. . . Sometimes this cleavage manifests itself in a superficial over-identification with everything American—an over-identification which disguises a profound alienation. Our past difficulties increase our present tendency toward such over-identification.'

Obviously, this desire to belong to the intellectual mainstream could be fulfilled in self-respecting ways which need not inhibit Catholics from attaining self-understanding. The result would then be an American intellectual tradition, creatively renewed and broadened by self-aware Catholics, in which Catholics and other Americans could find their places equally. John F. Kennedy had pointed the way.

For some, however, the desire to belong became an overriding determination to belong at all costs : in effect, to become like, and appear like, members of the central establishment of theorizers and literati, in the hope of winning entry into it. More specifically, this meant adopting the language, attitudes, prejudices, indignations, ideas, myths and manners of a loose-knit clerisy of new-style American puritans, generically termed liberal intellectuals, who have set the tone since the 1930's in the traditional heartland of American orthodoxy—the great cities and older universities of the East Coast.

Other impulses besides the desire to belong worked in the same direction : the general ambition of college-educated Catholics to *matter* in the intellectual field or what was deemed the intellectual field—to scale the only remaining height of American society still unscaled by the Catholic community; desires to be rid of cultural inferiority complex, to be freed from obsessive 'Catholic' feelings of depravity or guilt, to overcome feelings of weakness and emasculation. The prestige, influence, superiority complex and self-confidence of the establishment intellectuals—their tough, irreverent, contemptuous and even brutal tones—suggested a way of satisfying these desires by the easy method of uncritical imitation.

For those Catholics who took this way, such historical self-understanding as they might still want could only be illusion, not reality. It would have to conform to the necessities of the new belonging, strengthening wherever possible their bonds with this superficial Americanism, offering retrospective justification rather than true historical explanation. This was where the myth of the Irish came in, and this was why, once it had developed, it inhibited contradiction : it filled too many bills too well.

Dislike and contempt for the Irish are not new in America. Indeed, by propagating their myth of the Irish, the Catholic myth-makers joined a tradition that is at once native American and older than the United States. Its deep roots in the Anglo-Saxon cultural-religious tradition, and specifically in the dominant strain of that tradition—English Puritanism in its English and American variants—lend the myth a great deal of its force and significance.

Over a century ago Sydney Smith wrote of his fellow countrymen :

'The moment the very name of Ireland is mentioned, the English seem to bid adieu to common feeling, common prudence, and common sense, and to act with the barbarity of tyrants and the fatuity of idiots.'

It is no mere coincidence that, insofar as words are acts, this comment might seem to apply to the speech and writings of certain American Catholics over the past decade.

Before the Reformation, ordinary cultural antipathy and contempt had characterized the English attitude to the Irish—the documentary evidence abounds. After the Reformation, when the Irish remained Catholic, the worst English opinions on Irish mental and moral depravity seemed confirmed, and for none more so than the English Puritans, who established the American colonies and whose ideological descendants eventually dominated English culture at home.

Pointing out that Americans have inherited the basic qualities of their culture from the British, the American author Louis Wright, in *Culture on the Moving Frontier*[5] goes on to say :

'For that reason we need to take a long perspective of our history, a perspective which views America from at least the period of the first Tudor monarchs and lets us see the gradual development of our common civilization, its transmission across the Atlantic, and its expansion and modification as it was adapted to conditions in the Western hemisphere.'

Commenting on this passage in *American Catholicism*,[6] Mgr Tracy Ellis says :

'Americans are not Englishmen, but as Wright concludes, "we cannot escape an inheritance which has given us some of our sturdiest and most lasting qualities". Certainly the anti-Catholic bias brought to this country with the first English settlers has proved one of the sturdiest and most lasting of these qualities.'

Inevitably, for this Anglo-Saxon horror of Rome, the Irish, as the Romanists who were culturally nearest and most frequently encountered on both sides of the Atlantic, became the arch-Romanists, the Romanists *par excellence*; so that Irish and Catholic were felt to be synonymous. Besides, in the nineteenth century, American nativist sentiment against immigrants in general tended to concentrate on the Irish, drawing its fury from several sources at once.

[5] Harper and Row, New York.
[6] Doubleday, New York.

In his *Story of American Catholicism*,[7] Theodore Maynard writes :

'That resentment [on the part of the native Americans] was mainly turned against the Catholic Irish. The Germans, whether Catholics or Protestants, for the most part went off quietly to the West where, as they kept largely to themselves and retained their own language, they could be regarded as foreign colonies. But the Irish looked upon themselves as Americans from the moment they landed—a claim which seemed impudent to the older inhabitants.'

In the expanding English-speaking world of the nineteenth century, the Irish, themselves now English-speakers, became the 'outsiders' *par excellence*. Their extreme poverty, their thriftlessness, brashness and recklessness—qualities intolerable to puritans —contributed to this of course. Since the recent movement in American Catholicism has had a great deal to do with transforming 'outsider' status into 'insider' status, the deepest motivations and attractions of a myth which decries Irishness and calls for the rejection of everything 'Irish' in American Catholicism become readily intelligible.

Regardless of the slogans on its banners a Catholic movement which proclaims its Americanism by adapting an old American racial prejudice condemns itself as anti-intellectual and superficial —to say the least. The facile anti-Irishism is indeed only one of the signs that this movement is not a serious, creative participation in the best and most authentic values of the American heritage—which is what American Catholics seriously desire—but an opportunistic conforming to a shallow party line. Behind it lies the answer to a question about recent American Catholic soul-searching which has puzzled casual listeners-in : why, if American Catholics are, on the one hand, eager to join the American mainstream and, on the other, concerned about religious authoritarianism, anti-intellectualism and old-style puritanism, has their discussion of these characteristics of their lives shown so little awareness of obvious counterparts in American history and culture? Even a casual delving into the most authentic American

[7] 2 vols, Doubleday Image, New York.

tradition reveals religious and other authoritarianism, anti-intellectualism and old-style puritanism at every turn.

Obviously, if American Catholics are to achieve the historical self-understanding which they need if they are to overcome their cultural defects, play a creative role in American intellectual life, and contribute important insight to the Catholic Church as a whole, they cannot remain stuck in the blind alley of the Irish scapegoat myth. Nor is it probable they will remain there. The Irish myth has succeeded because it was an excitingly useful, almost necessary, component of what seemed like an entry by shortcut into the inner sanctum of the American psyche. The creative intellectual fusion with the American tradition which is really wanted—a fusion which must inevitably transform that tradition—matures more slowly. It may be already under way.

This much is clear however : the Irish scapegoat myth is a betrayal of the best interests of American Catholics. It has thwarted self-understanding, and this damage must be repaired. In seeking the historical genesis of the late Tridentine ills of the American church, American Catholic scholarship could well have afforded to by-pass nineteenth-century Irish Catholicism, or to have been satisfied with a glance in that direction. Now, however, that the Irish myth has secured credence and befogged the view, Catholic scholarship must see the clearing up of this distracting illusion as an imperative preliminary task. Done well, this scholarly labour would provide fresh insights of self-understanding to English-speaking Catholicism as a whole and thus repay, incidentally and in some measure, the outstanding debt of the American Church to the Church in Ireland.

11

THE MODERN MISSIONARY MOVEMENT[1]

Size and extent

The Easter Rising of 1916, of which the fiftieth anniversary was celebrated last year, was a sharp turning-point in modern Irish history. Later in the same year, on 10 October 1916, the establishment of the Maynooth Mission to China indicated another turning-point, more gradual in contour but of at least equal importance. In the special, conventional sense of the word missions, meaning organized missions to non-Christians, the modern Irish missionary movement can be said to have got under way with this venture.

There is a common misconception, especially on the European continent, that Ireland has always been a 'great missionary country'. As a matter of fact, however, missionary work proper has been an outstanding feature of the Catholic Church in Ireland only in the early Christian centuries (especially the seventh and eighth) and again in the present century. From the late eighteenth century onwards, Irish Catholic migration, as well as Irish priests, sisters, brothers and bishops, had been extending and building up the Church in all the countries of the English-speaking world. But large-scale evangelical effort directed towards non-Christian peoples did not develop until the decades following the First World War. This missionary movement followed in the wake of the Irish revolution, somewhat as other kinds of missionary and expansive movements followed the French and Russian revolution. It was part of a general upsurge of vitality

[1] July 1967.

which expressed itself in various ways and was reflected in the more than doubling of the crude rate of natural increase in the country between 1911-19 and the late 1950s. The two major, parallel enterprises of the Irish Catholic people during these decades were state-building and far-flung missionary activity.

The first of six Irish missionary foundations between 1916 and 1952, the Maynooth Mission to China, was co-founded by Fr Edward Galvin, who had already spent four years in China, and Fr John Blowick, a professor from Maynooth College. It later acquired a second name, the Society of St Columban, or the Columban Fathers. Today the society numbers over a thousand priests and students, and has 560 members on active work on the missions. They were ejected from China in 1951 and today their largest concentration is 166 members in the Philippines, with 99 in Korea, 78 in Japan, 29 in Burma, 18 in Fiji, 14 in Peru, 11 in Chile and 1 in Formosa. (Most, though not all, of the missionary statistics in this article have been taken from a 'Statistical Analysis of the Irish Missionary Effort Overseas' compiled between February 1964 and May 1965. They should be regarded as approximations.)

Like many missionary priests before them, the Columbans felt the need for the cooperation of women religious if their work was to affect the population in depth. In 1922 Fr Blowick founded the Missionary Sisters of St Columban to work with the fathers. By 1926 the sisters were in China. Ejected with the other missionaries, they today have 116 members on the mission fields. Their largest concentration is also in the Philippines where 51 sisters are engaged in social and educational work. In Korea 30 sisters operate general and TB clinics and hospitals. There are 22 sisters in Hong Kong, 8 in Burma and 5 in Peru.

The other four Irish missionary foundations of the twentieth century were aimed at Africa, largely due to the influence of two famous Irish missionaries already at work in Africa for many years, Bishop Joseph Shanahan, C.S.Sp., of Southern Nigeria, and Mother Kevin of Uganda. Bishop Shanahan's fame as a pioneer is linked with his plan of 1905 to push out from the known trading routes and posts and cover his entire territory with a network of Catholic schools, thus creating the conditions for a future viable Christian community. He founded the third of the new Irish missionary societies, the Holy Rosary Sisters of Killeshandra, in 1924, to complement the work of his Holy Ghost fathers. Today more than 216 Holy Rosary sisters work on the mission fields in Nigeria, Cameroons, Sierra Leone, Kenya and Transvaal, as teachers, doctors, nurses, laboratory technicians, chemists, radiographers, secretaries, social workers. They run hospitals, dispensaries and clinics, train nurses, and teach from infant school to teacher training colleges and marriage preparation level.

The next foundation, in 1932, St Patrick's Foreign Missionary Society, better known as the Kiltegan Fathers, sprang indirectly from Bishop Shanahan's influence. In answer to his appeal for help, the Irish bishops had allowed diocesan priests to spend a few years as volunteers in Nigeria. Some years' experience pointed to the need for a home organization to secure and regulate a steady supply, and St Patrick's Society was founded, though volunteers still help out. The society has grown to around 400 priests and students and has over 190 priests at work in Africa and 4 in South America.

The fifth missionary foundation, the Medical Missionaries of Mary, founded in 1937, also owes something to Bishop Shanahan's influence. The founder of the Medical Missionaries, Marie Martin, was one of a group of young girls who went to Nigeria in 1920 in answer to another bishop's appeals for help. She soon found that her vocation was to bring adequate medical services to Africans, and especially a maternity service. At that time Catholic religious were not allowed to practise gynaecology or obstetrics. Miss Martin worked and waited until in 1936 permission was granted and the Medical Missionaries could get under way. Their apostolate is specifically a medical one, and the 108 members in the field in Nigeria, Tanzania, Angola, Nyasaland, Uganda, Kenya and Ethiopia run a network of modern hospitals, while at their headquarters in Drogheda, north of Dublin, they maintain a first-class international training hospital. The thoroughly modern, innovating spirit of the Medical Missionaries was reflected from the start in the simplified, practical habit worn by the sisters. It antedated by more than twenty years the present movement of reform in the dress of women religious.

The sixth foundation, the Franciscan Missionary Sisters for Africa, was made in 1952 by the famous 'Mama Kevina' of Uganda. Born Teresa Kearney in Co Wicklow, she joined the Franciscan Sisters of the Five Wounds at Mill Hill, London, and arrived in Uganda with their first pioneering group in 1903. There she built up their mission and eventually, driven by perennial inability to get sufficient personnel from her own order in England, got permission to erect its African province into a new order with its mother house at Dundalk. Today there are 120 sisters at work in Uganda, Kenya, Rhodesia and South Africa. They are engaged in social work and in education from kindergarten to teacher training, including the teaching of the handicapped. They run general and maternity hospitals, clinics and dispensaries, two leprosaria and a recognized training school for state-enrolled nurses and midwives. Not the least of Mother Kevin's achievements was the foundation of an order of African nuns, the Little Sisters of St Francis. Incidentally, she herself was the first nun to get a training in midwifery.

In the 1950s the number of lay professional people from Ireland engaged in mission work began to rise steeply towards its present level of approximately 500. Several societies have been founded by laypeople to organize and encourage missionary outlets for doctors, nurses, teachers, architects and others.

The development of all these new societies has been accompanied by an equally great expansion among the older missionary bodies in Ireland. For example, the Irish province of the Holy Ghost Fathers, the Irish congregation with the largest numbers of priests on the mission field, had 143 members in 1920, 620 in 1959. The Irish province of the Society of African Missions, SMA, in 1920 numbered 40 members and by 1959 had reached over 400.

The 'Statistical Analysis' published by the Missionary Service Centre in Dublin in 1965 was based on figures supplied by 92 mission-sending bodies in Ireland. It gives the following tables :

Continent	Priests	Brothers	Sisters	Laity	Totals
AFRICA	1,443	230	2,004	445	4,122
ASIA AND OCEANIA	651	257	1,047	7	1,962
LATIN AMERICA	210	54	139	30	433
TOTALS	2,304	541	3,190	482	6,517

Priests ordained for English-speaking countries overseas :

College	Great Britain	Australia and New Zealand	North America	South Africa
ALL HALLOWS, DUBLIN	380	360	436	45
IRISH COLLEGE, ROME	17	24	21	5
ST KIERAN'S, KILKENNY	314	107	189	4
ST PATRICK'S, THURLES	142	100	246	33
ST PATRICK'S, CARLOW	269	131	533	10
ST PETER'S, WEXFORD	139	42	112	
TOTALS	1,261	764	1,537	97

Sum total 3,659, but the real total is larger since figures from St John's College, Waterford, are not included.

To put these figures into some perspective, it is worth noting that about two years ago there were over 5,963 Irish priests working abroad as against 5,984 priests (diocesan and all others) at home. Over 50% of all priests ordained in Ireland in any year go directly abroad. The Catholic population of Ireland is three and a quarter million.

The steep rise in the numbers of Irish missionary personnel in the years 1920-60 was itself part of a rapid and continuous increase, from the 1880s onward, in ordinations to the priesthood and commitments to the religious life. Between 1871 and 1961, despite a fall of 25% in the Catholic population, the number of diocesan priests working in Ireland rose from 2,655 to 3,027, the number of other priests from 406 to 2,016. This resulted in a priest/people ratio of 1:861 for diocesan priests, 1:558 for all priests, a great improvement on ninety years before. In a sense, then, the missionary movement represented the efforts of a superfluity of ecclesiastical personnel to find outlets for their energies in a situation where home needs were being adequately catered for and the traditional flow of clergy and religious to the English-speaking countries was being strongly maintained.

Only in the past few years has this pattern of general increase shown any signs of changing. A slight decrease in entries to seminaries and a sharp fall in the perseverance ratio of priest candidates were experienced first by the missionary societies, later by the seminaries in general. It is still too early to see what is happening. The old pattern may be restored, a new one may be emerging. Part of the cause for the decline in entries to seminaries has been a stiffening of the criteria for admission.

As the above tables show, Africa has the largest contingent of Irish missionaries of the three areas, 4,122 spread over 27 countries. Nigeria leads the field with 748 priests, 408 sisters, 13 brothers and 388 laity.

This concentration in Nigeria is accidental, not planned, in the sense that it did not develop according to a preconceived plan but piecemeal in answer to various appeals. The pattern is repeated throughout the whole field of Irish missionary effort. Generally speaking it developed in response to particular needs at particular times. Thus there is another large concentration in South Africa where an Irish bishop, Dr Grimley, brought the Irish Dominican sisters in 1863. Here there are 879 nuns, with 161 priests and 126 brothers. Numerically Kenya comes next with 202 priests, 184 sisters, 4 Patrician Brothers and 5 laymen, and then Uganda with 14 priests, 91 sisters and three laypeople.

In Asia the largest concentration of Irish priests is in the Philippines, where there are 244. There are 61 in Hong Kong, 99 in Korea, 81 in Japan, 61 in India, 29 in Burma, 27 in Fiji and smaller numbers in Malaysia, Borneo, Indonesia, Iran, Pakistan, Solomons, Tonga, Vietnam and Thailand. Of the 1,962 Irish nuns in Asia and Oceania the largest number is in India where Loreto and Presentation nuns have been working since the 1840s. India has 321 sisters, Pakistan 178, Malaysia 121, Ceylon 115, Philippines 78, Borneo 48, Burma 44, Japan 34, Korea 35. There are smaller numbers in the Fiji (30), Cook and Gilbert Islands, Formosa, Indonesia, Hong Kong, Middle East, Vietnam and Thailand, Papua and New Guinea, New Caledonia and Solomons.

Of the 257 brothers, 150 are in India, 33 in Malaysia, 24 in Hong Kong, and smaller numbers in the Philippines, Borneo, Korea, Burma, Pakistan and Vietnam.

In Latin America by far the largest number of Irish missionaries is in Trinidad, where the Irish connection goes back for hundreds of years. Here there are 78 priests, 50 nuns, and 12 Presentation Brothers. The rest of the West Indies has 28 Sisters of St Joseph of Cluny and 19 Presentation Brothers. Irish emigrants and priests have been in the West Indies since at least the seventeenth century and the present missionary groups are established there since the nineteenth century.

On the continent of South America the Irish effort is only getting under way. While the work being done in this area is for the most part not missionary in the strict sense, since most of South America has been at least superficially christianized, nevertheless the extreme pastoral neglect throughout huge areas has turned them into missionary areas de facto. In no country does the Church possess a pastoral structure which is anything like adequate. Argentina has 29 priests, 20 nuns, 13 Christian Brothers, and 4 lay missionaries. Brazil has 37 priests, 11 nuns, 2 brothers and 8 lay people, Chile 17 priests, 19 nuns, 13 Christian Brothers and 4 lay people, and Peru 40 priests, 7 nuns, 4 lay people. There are smaller representations in Uruguay, Venezuela, Paraguay, Mexico, Bolivia, Columbia, Costa Rica, Ecuador, Guatemala and Guinea.

When we try to compare the number of Irish missionaries with those of other leading missionary countries we run into difficulties, as there does not seem to be any central statistical agency. A recent enquiry to the International Fides Service of the Propaganda at Rome could only elicit the following figures of priests serving overseas: Dutch 4,392, US 3,946, Belgian 3,603, Canadian 1,537, Swiss 657. These figures refer to all priests serving overseas, and not only to those in technically mission areas, and so may be compared with the total of 5,963 Irish priests serving abroad.

The most that we can conclude is that Ireland and the Netherlands are, numerically speaking, probably the leading mission-sending countries relative to Catholic population. The Missionary Service Centre in Dublin may be congratulated on its complete and informative analysis of the numbers of all Irish ecclesiastical personnel working overseas.

The historical background

After the great missionary effort of the seventh, eighth and, to a lesser extent, the eleventh centuries, when Irishmen helped to evangelize the pagan tribes of Europe, nearly a thousand years passed without Ireland making any substantial contribution to the evangelization of the non-Christian world. There were reasons for this, notably the Norman invasion of 1169 and the succeeding centuries of gradual extension of Anglo-Norman control. The Reformation left invaders and invaded sharply divided by religion. This troubled period culminated at the end of the seventeenth century in what seemed the final conquest, which placed all civil and military power in Protestant and largely alien hands and was accompanied by the passing of the famous 'penal laws' which to a large extent outlawed both Catholics and their religion.

However, the more or less surreptitious practice of the Catholic religion was tolerated, with occasional punitive outbursts. Since trade and commerce were among the few areas open to Catholics, a Catholic middle-class emerged, wealthy enough to educate their children in Catholic schools overseas or sometimes at home in the few Catholic schools that managed to survive. Towards the close of the century, when the laws were relaxed and Catholic religious societies began to appear, there seems to have been no critical shortage of educated middle-class recruits.

The new religious societies enjoyed an uneasy toleration based on government fears of worse evil resulting from the continued education of Catholics, and especially students for the priesthood, in revolutionary Europe. Maynooth College owed its origin to this fear. Some of the new religious societies were of Irish origin : the Presentation Sisters, founded in 1775; the Irish Christian Brothers and Presentation Brothers, both springing from an original foundation in 1802; the Irish Sisters of Charity, founded 1815; the Irish Sisters of Mercy, 1831, being among the first.

Others came from abroad : the Ursulines in 1771, the Rosminians in 1831, the Vincentians in 1835, and many more. They shared the same objective : to serve the underprivileged Irish, to provide more priests, education for rich and poor, services for the poor, the old, sick, the homeless and the orphaned.

At the same time schools ostensibly founded to give secondary education quietly developed into seminaries. Without delay, these new seminaries were drawn into extending their services overseas in those areas where Irish emigrants were already settled in numbers, and by the end of the nineteenth century there were six major seminaries sending the large majority of the priests they ordained overseas. This trend was already established before the great famine of the 1840s turned the flow of emigration into a torrent and sent inceasing numbers of Irish priests all over the English-speaking world to serve the needs of the Irish immigrants and of other Catholics.

Wherever they found need for schools, hospitals or other social services, Irish-born bishops and priests were likely to look to Ireland for help. The new Irish congregations of sisters and brothers were hardly established before they were drawn into overseas service.

Meanwhile the old-established orders of Europe, the Dominicans, Franciscans, Augustinians, Capuchins and Jesuits, had been carrying on the missionary work proper. In Africa the old Catholic missions struggled to survive during the eighteenth century in the face of the crippling death rate among Europeans in Africa. In the Far East, since the palmy days of the Jesuits at the imperial court of Peking, the missions were fighting a losing battle against hostility and indifference. The nineteenth century saw a mighty resurgence of Christian missionary effort, Catholic and Protestant, of nearly all west European nationalities, and now Americans as well. The French revolution no doubt contributed a release of energy, and among Catholic missionaries it was especially a French effort, but the movement as a whole was closely connected with the race for colonies and spheres of influence in Africa and the East which involved most of the countries of Western Europe and the United States.

Feelings of responsibility for the exploited peoples gave an impetus to the missionary drive to supply Christianity and various kinds of charitable work, while interdenominational and international rivalry also played their parts. Colonial officials on the spot were inclined to use the missionaries as the most efficient and cheapest means available of extending the then unquestioned benefits of western civilization. As Britain gradually came out on top in the struggle for commercial supremacy, the non-English-speaking Catholic missionary bodies looked more and more to Ireland for personnel. The Irish were doubly suitable as they both spoke English and were familiar with the niceties of Catholic existence under British rule.

So in Ireland the two trends towards service throughout the English-speaking world and towards missionary work proper in the non-Christian world developed side by side and interacted. There was an interesting nineteenth-century connection between Maynooth College and the sees of Madras and Calcutta. Several Irish bishops drew considerable numbers of Irish priests to India and were responsible for bringing the Presentation and Loreto Sisters in the 1840s and later the Patrician Brothers, the Irish Christian Brothers and the Irish De La Salle Brothers. The 'Maynooth Mission to India' petered out in 1911 due to lack of organization at home. In Africa, the modern missionary period is dated from the arrival in Liberia from the USA in 1842 of three Irishmen led by Bishop Barron, a product of St John's College, Waterford, one of the six seminaries previously mentioned which sent, and still send, the great majority of their priests all over the English-speaking world. As already mentioned, it was an Irish bishop, Dr Grimley, who brought the Irish Dominican sisters to South Africa in 1863.

This was how Irish involvement in Africa and Asia began. Irish bishops, often sent to these continents via England or the USA, drew some of their fellow-countrymen, priests, sisters and brothers, after them. Missionary congregations from the European continent, and especially from France, established themselves in Ireland and began to win recruits: the Holy Ghost Fathers in 1859, the Sisters of St Joseph of Cluny in 1860, the Society of African Missions in 1878. The White Fathers did not make an establishment until 1955 and have few Irish members today.

But in the nineteenth century and, indeed, until the third decade of the twentieth century, very few Irish were engaged in the direct evangelization of non-Christian peoples. Most of the priests, sisters and brothers who went to Africa or Asia were either administrators or schoolteachers who worked in the major cities and largely among the white colonial population and the more assimilated, partly christianized, sections of the native peoples. The continental missionary societies in Ireland won recruits slowly and did not engage in any substantial missionary work abroad; they got involved in the immediately pressing needs of the Irish church, which was engaged in the great task of rebuilding itself from the bottom up. They contributed by founding schools and in other ways. For their proper work they had to wait by and large until the mood of the country changed towards the end of the second decade of the present century. The Columban Fathers lit the decisive spark.

Meanwhile the interest of the public was being fostered by the introduction of the new movement 'for the propagation of the faith', which involved the laity by committing them to prayer for the missions and to a small weekly donation. The First World War, by causing many missionaries to return to Europe and halting the flow of replacements, resulted in numbers of Irish being called on to fill the vacancies.

Achievement—and new challenge

When the Irish missionary movement was getting under way, the primary aim of the missionaries, as of all previous and contemporary Christian missionaries, was to baptize non-Christians. In a curious book which reflects the mentality and practice current among European missionaries in Africa around 1920, James Mellett, C.S.Sp., one of the Irish pioneers, tells of arduous journeys from village to village for the express purpose of baptizing dying infants.[2] By the 1930s the emphasis had shifted from dying infants to living adults and children : schools and hospitals had become the focal activities of missionaries. In this shift from

[2] *Let No Man Dare*, Dublin, 1964.

the last-minute rescue for the other world to systematic social service for this world, the Irish missionaries played a leading role. But the overriding aim remained as before : baptism.

Millions were baptized, Christian communities grew. In Nigeria, which has experienced the heaviest concentration of Irish missionaries, the Catholic population increased from 163,000 in 1920 to 2,390,666 in 1965. Missionary success was reckoned primarily in numbers of baptisms, but also in the moving evidence of the Spirit at work in the individual Christian lives of Africans and Asians. (This was measured numerically in terms of candidates for the priesthood and girls taking the sister's veil.) As the primary criterion of missionary success was numerical, so, too, in the recruiting of missionaries from home, the first emphasis was on numbers : as many as possible as quickly as possible, for there was a whole world to win for Christ. The second urgent requirement from home was money. Here, too, the criterion was quantity.

Zealous propagandists, equipped with films, slides and brochures, criss-crossed Ireland again and again. With the moving eloquence of witnesses to the dire needs of Africa and Asia and to the high spiritual adventure of the missionary's life, they spoke to school classes, church congregations and audiences in parish halls. A vast missionary press developed. In its contents and distribution (largely by promoters in schools, factories and big commercial and public offices) it was tailored to the hard-sell of the same two requirements : recruits and money. Money was given generously, thousands answered the call for personal commitment, and in the seminaries and novitiates of the missionary societies the young men and women, fired by their returned older colleagues, could not wait to be gone.

The millions who came under the influence of the missionaries received much more from them than baptism, schooling and medical care. They acquired a sense of individual dignity and a new, enlarged vision of life's possibilities. Fair dealing as between persons, according to rationally discernible criteria, became part of their experience and expectations. The dynamic unease of modern Europe, its ambition to control and transform the material world, entered into their lives. The possibilities of personal moral advance and of an intimate I-Thou relationship with God were opened to many for the first time. Women's status and sense of self-worth were enhanced. Many crippling shackles of witchcraft, superstition and religious fear were thrown off. In some places, sex relations between man and wife were humanized, becoming at once less animal and less mysterious.

In recent years it is becoming clear to the Irish, as to all Christian missionaries, that the policy dominated by criteria of number and quantity is running into trouble at both ends. Millions have been baptized but, relative to population, and especially to rapidly increasing populations, the Christians in Africa and Asia are still few. At the same time recruitments to the missionary societies among the home population has been strained to its limits; a decline has set in. Money is still assured— it is available in potentially greater quantity than ever before. But the question now arises : what policy or programme, with what goals and governed by what criteria, should the money be made to serve ?

It is not only the iron logic of numbers that urges a rethinking of missionary work from the bottom up. The accumulated results of the missionaries' efforts—Christians baptized, institutions established, people culturally uprooted and communally disrupted —have contributed to the policy dilemma, causing the simple aim of baptizing as many as possible to recede into the background by sheer logic of circumstances. Moreover, the new self-governing states, which have resulted in an indirect way from European missionary activity as a whole, have produced situations and challenges which did not exist previously.

Catholic communities have grown in size to become churches in their own right. Since they lack an adequate supply of native clergy and religious, missionary personnel have had to be diverted to them from the missionary 'frontier'. The slowness of Irish priests, as distinct from sisters and brothers, to promote recruitment of colleagues from among the native populations is coming home to roost.

At the same time, the growing scale of missionary involvement in social service has had a similar effect. Desacralized, regarded in its secular dimension and according to the ordinary non-religious criteria of the present age, the Irish missionary movement represents what is probably the greatest contribution, proportionate to population, of any western people to the 'underdeveloped countries'. The point is, however, that these networks of schools, teacher training colleges, hospitals and clinics, with their ancillary services of counselling and material aid, exert their own demands, for their own continuance and expansion, on the personnel resources of the missionary bodies which have sponsored them.

Then again, as children have reached maturity, as secondary schools succeeded primary schools to be followed in turn by institutes of higher education, as cities have grown and rural populations have been transformed into urban-dwellers, as the new Catholics have become citizens of self-governing states, the qualities, skills and knowledge required in missionaries have become more specific, differentiated and sophisticated. Due to indifference on the part of the missionaries to the cultural implications of their activity, to the historical situations in which it was being conducted and to the political developments going on around them, these ignored elements of reality have now materialized as problems. Proletarization due to cultural and social dislocation, uneasy relationships with the new civil authorities and inadequate Catholic political leadershp have resulted in situations which threaten the growth and continuance of the Church.

Broadly speaking, more is now required from the missionaries than previously, but this 'more' is a 'more' of quality. Moral quality being assumed, the emphatic need is now for those qualities which derive from relevant secular learning and learned skills, from knowledge of historical situation and culture, and from awareness of the values and requirements of citizenship. Men and women are needed who possess a reflective understanding of self, people and Church as embodiments of culture in a concrete historical and political situation.

Apart from the unknowable role of the Holy Spirit, the Irish missionary movement hitherto has been a combination of Irish vitality, generosity, skill in human relations, intellectual incuriosity and general mental uncultivatedness with Anglo-Saxon pragmatism. Its predominant spirit has been that of the man who hacks his way into a burning house to rescue people trapped there, the spirit of people rebuilding their homes in winter after a storm has levelled them. Unreflective, rushing to answer call after call of dire need, working under the tyrannous pressure of necessities seen as urgent and unlimited, the Irish missionaries have not paused to get to know themselves and the specific culture, with all its peculiarities and assumptions, which they brought with them and embodied. They have not taken time off to survey the human landscape of their endeavours, to study its contours. Many questions have remained unasked about the goal of their efforts—not in heaven but on earth, not in terms of a spiritual reality which for the most part can only be guessed at, but in terms of the total, adequately knowable lives and cultures of the people to whom they are addressing themselves, not in a timeless age, but in this present age of their own and of other people's history.

Small wonder then, given this unwillingness to look at, study and see life, that the Irish missionary movement has produced no literature worth mentioning : no books describing the peoples encountered, no travellers' tales told in a spirit of wonder and enquiry, no history of the missionary movement itself or of any broad part of it, no general reflections on Africa or Asia, no journal (let alone books) of ethnology, comparative religion or missiology. When one recalls the literary impact on the home country of any similar major exodus of Europeans to distant lands and strange cultures, the relative silence of the Irish missionaries can only be termed unnatural.

The house-on-fire spirit, the emergency mentality, leads inevitably to narrow-sighted activism. Fortunately for Africa and Asia the narrow-mindedness of the missionaries was not of the kind that constrains the heart. The emergency mentality which blinkered them, and induced them to remain so, was part and parcel of modern Irish Catholicism as a whole, an ideological heritage from its formative period in the nineteenth century. Then, a people whose own culture and historic community were broken and who faced urgent necessity at every turn had to find a world-view that would make life possible in their desperate circumstances.

By fusing two highly individualistic outlooks, the melancholy, blinkered world-view of late Tridentine Catholicism with the myopic utilitarianism and mental insulation of Victorian Britain, they had found an ideology that fitted their plight. It was this fusion, in conditions of extreme need, of late Tridentine Catholic with modern Anglo-Saxon attitudes and values that produced, first in Ireland, then elsewhere, that activist, narrow-sighted ideology of modern English-speaking Catholicism which in Catholic circles on the continent of Europe is sometimes called 'American' and 'materialistic'.

In nineteenth-century Catholic Ireland, with its cultural dislocation, social disintegration and extreme material needs, this ideology was grimly useful because it battered down despair and got basic things done. The trouble was that it conditioned the people who used it into accepting it as a 'normal' way of regarding life and the world, as a 'normal' way of living. Even worse, it conditioned them into *needing* it to make life seem purposeful. Since it forbade reflection or real awareness, it involved ignoring the cultural and social disruption which was at the root of it, the extreme emergency which had made such a crassly inhuman approach to life and the world the best of a bad bargain.

On the impossible hypothesis that the Irish missionaries had become aware, before setting out, of the utterly disjointed situation in which they and their people found themselves, they might perhaps have taken care to set their own socio-cultural house in order first, or at least have gone out to Africa and Asia conscious that they embodied a cultural sickness which, if communicated, could disrupt the lives of their would-be converts as their own lives had been disrupted. On this impossible hypothesis, they could have gone out as experts (in the most literal sense) in socio-cultural health and dislocation and thus have lessened and counteracted the cultural harm that was being done in Africa and Asia by Europeans in general. As it was, they went out unaware, more as zealous, generous, blind automata than as conscious men, adding to, rather than counteracting the cultural and social disruption of the peoples whom they thought they loved but could not—since they never opened their minds to their lives nor sought to know them for their own sakes.

'Materialistic' is an inadequate description of the Catholic ideology which the missionaries inherited; but it is inadequate merely because one-sided and because it judges by appearances only. What looks to outsiders like 'materialism' was often experienced as a very 'spiritual' way of thinking and acting by those involved. At the bottom of it all was a profound pessimism about man in his earthly life, a pessimism which reflected a deep-down intuition common to the age and which was reinforced by contemporary religious ideas and by Irish history. This pessimism, fearing the worst from enquiry into human life, inhibited its victims from using their mental faculties to wonder about, investigate, observe and reflect upon themselves, others, human life and language, man. Thus minds were thwarted in their integrating, humanizing function. There was a 'spiritual realm' of frozen ideas about eternal values and about a statically conceived world, there was the 'material world' of everyday action, unrelated to the 'spiritual realm'. Life had to go on in both of them simultaneously. It was inhuman, but the alternative, integration, would have involved looking at life whole and reflecting on it—and this was out.

By the 1920s in Ireland, in every sphere except the intellectual, the epic period of Catholic struggle and rebuilding was past. The Catholic people in most of the country had taken their political future into their own hands. In the other English-speaking countries, which continued to provide an outlet for the zeal of Irish priests and religious, the material emergency was also past, the period of Catholic consolidation was setting in. In a sense, then, the missionaries, though practical innovators, were extreme conservatives. Faced with a situation where a new mentality was demanded, they turned away from it to rediscover the old tyranny of material necessity, the old ready-made, mind-numbing purposefulness in the limitless needs of Africa and Asia.

The missionaries set off to encounter these strange peoples knowing little more of them, and feeling they need know little

more, than that they had different-coloured skin, engaged in re-
prehensible practices and had souls that needed saving, heads
that needed the water of baptism. Gradually they took into
account their bodies that needed healing, their minds that needed
book-learning.

These elementary facts and needs were seen and thought of
piecemeal : there was no systematic, genuinely interested study
of the cultures, religions and historical situations of these peoples,
no thought of their all-round needs as communities and as persons. Nor did the first years of missionary experience lead to
systematic study of such matters either in the mission countries
or at home; such learning as was done was of the ad hoc kind,
in response to immediate, crudely observed needs. As for the fact
that the missionaries departed, and still depart, without any
course of study in modern European or modern Anglo-Saxon
culture—and thus without adequate self-knowledge—this is
hardly surprising when, to this day, in the venerable seminaries
that have prepared priests for the English-speaking mission for
a hundred and fifty years, no course is given in the history of
English-speaking culture in the nineteenth and twentieth
centuries.

The missionaries' deficient awareness in the cultural field and
their insensitivity to man's socio-cultural requirements mitigated
against the enduring efficacy of their work. But they were also
at a disadvantage because of their insensitivity to political or civil
history, especially in respect of citizenship, its values and its role
in human life.

As it happens, this factor has been of increasing importance in
Africa and Asia in recent decades; since the end of the Second
World War its importance there has been crucial. Because of
their insensitivity to citizenship as a value, the missionaries failed
to integrate considerations of approaching citizenship and political
self-determination in their teaching and training activities. As a
result, their flocks are generally deficient in political acumen and
in qualities of leadership. More unfortunate still, by their frequently reserved and apprehensive attitude to the national independence movements—by failing to go along with them in time
—they have made it more difficult for relations of confidence to

be established between the new régimes on the one hand, the Church and its works on the other. At the same time this coolness *vis-à-vis* the self-government movements had addled in varying degrees the relationship of Catholics to the states of which they have now become citizens.

At first glance, in view of the course of Irish history in the present century, it might seem that Irishmen, of all people, would be especially conscious of the values and implications of citizenship in a self-governing nation state. But this expectation would leave out of account the continuing influence on the Irish church of the 'revolution from Rome' which transformed it in the mid-nineteenth century. Specifically, it would leave out of account the degree to which that ultramontane movement alienated, in an enduring manner, the clerical and specially consecrated elements of the Catholic people from their civil and political elements. Contrary to what is often assumed in anti-Catholic circles abroad, the clerical elements of the Church in Ireland did not, by and large, either work for or rejoice over the establishment of a self-governing Irish state (so that they would dominate the people in civil matters as they were already doing in religious, and so on). The clerical element tended by and large to look askance at the new civil community and its institutions; when not openly suspicious, their attitude towards them, as evidenced by words and actions, by silence and inaction, was less than generous or fraternal.

The missionaries, being ecclesiastically conservative, fell inevitably under this spell. Except for the earlier pioneers, they had every opportunity, growing up in Ireland and receiving their education there, to sense themselves as what they in fact were—citizens of a new state that was vigorously asserting its right to statehood. Schooling in citizenship and in the establishment of self-government was available to them. That they lacked civic awareness, that they suppressed this dimension of personality, that they did not act as citizens among citizens but merely as clerics or religious and as members of their particular missionary congregation, was due to the inhibiting ecclesiastical ideology to which they adhered. Their inhibitions in this respect were to hinder their work in Africa and Asia when, by living out their Irish citizenship and their recent history in the home country, they could have benefited their mission. Faced by the need today to make wider demands on the home country than ever before, their past inhibitions in regard to citizenship and their continuing hesitance in overcoming them have placed obstacles in their way on the home front also.

The future health of the Church in Africa and Asia depends on the degree to which these peoples, including the Christians among them, achieve cultural health and civil cohesion with freedom and justice. It depends on how well the Christians, as effective citizens and members of the cultural community, are integrated into the civil societies of which they form part. Obviously, then, the future service of the Irish missionary bodies to these peoples requires that they procure the dispatch of men and women who understand these tasks and can help in them. This will involve a broadening and deepening of the education of missionaries. It will also mean equipping many more of them than hitherto with special kinds of professional knowledge and with special skills. Indeed, many of the new missionaries, if they are to match up to what is required by the situation, will be not so much like the old missionaries as like community-development experts, professional people or academic specialists, of prayerful Christian life.

When this is accepted, the question arises of how such people are to be produced and how large numbers of them are to be induced to go to Africa, Asia and, indeed, South America. Linked to this is the other question of how priests and religious, whose work will consist largely in carrying out parish duties and staffing existing social services, will receive a basic formation in the hitherto neglected dimensions. Clearly, what is now required goes beyond the resources of seminaries and novitiates and exceeds in scope the existing methods of supplementary missionary training. The Missionary Service Centre, founded in Dublin in 1961, with Fr Michael Pelly, S.J., in charge, has organized several summer courses for missionaries which covered a wide variety of topics. But this work, however laudable, is merely a stop-gap, a pointer towards what needs to be done. The entire educational resources of an advanced society would need to be drawn on, and these resources would need to include research institutes and schools dealing specifically with the cultures of Africa and Asia and with their special contemporary problems.

Insofar as it is a question of money and of building on an existing educational structure, Ireland could supply what is needed. Teachers would need to be brought in, additional finance might need to be sought abroad; but these things could be done. However, if what is required for such a refurbished programme is to be made available in Ireland, the missionary societies will need to transform their relationship to Irish society. They will also need to address themselves to it as a whole and to find means of making their work and their vision seem relevant and important to all sections of the civil and cultural community.

For reasons that must be obvious from what has been said already, Irish society has not been culturally or intellectually enriched by the missionary movement. Its consciousness has not been broadened or deepened, its fund of learning hardly increased; no vision has been offered to it. The universities contain no institutes of African or Asian studies, have no chairs of comparative religion or ethnology. The missionaries have not contributed schools teaching these subjects, nor have they presented the nation with an ethnological museum. The Medical Missionaries of Mary have established a hospital for tropical diseases at Drogheda. A Dublin printer and publisher turns out books in several African languages. Over the years some thousands of students from the mission territories have attended Irish universities. Apart from such isolated instances, there has been little to show.

Hitherto the missionaries have not addressed themselves to the Irish public in general. They have not reported back to the society which produced, educated and financed them, and which allowed them to share in the graces of its Christian life. In the first place, this was because they had nothing of broadly human interest to say (if they had, they would have said it, have written it down in books). Secondly, this omission was due to the fact that they did not speak with a common voice. On the whole, the mission-sending bodies have worked separately from each other pursuing their activities in a particularistic manner, hardly ex-

changing experience and ideas. The appeals for support have
come from individual missionary societies and from individual
members of these societies. A breakthrough in this respect has
been effected by the Missionary Service Centre, to which thirty
of them are affiliated and which is inducing them to come together more.

Then again, the self-presentation of the missionary bodies to
the Catholic people at home was very much a hole and corner
affair. They addressed themselves not to the people at large or
to the body of fellow citizens, but largely to schoolchildren, to
their respective groups of votaries and to their own families.
Whatever public their magazines were directed to—and these
were as numerous as the mission-sending bodies themselves—it
was certainly not the adult male public or the intelligent female
one, not the men of affairs nor the professionals of the mass media
and of news dissemination. Vitiating the impact of all the missionaries' appeals, whether by magazine or by word of mouth,
was the narrow concentration on recruits, money and prayers.
The vast majority of people were not interested in joining, money
was easily given and forgotten. The narrow range of the missionaries' own interests frustrated people's ability to be interested
in them or their work. In a word, the missions were not made
relevant to the ordinary life and daily concerns of Irish society,
they remained utterly marginal.

How little impact on public consciousness this fifty year old
movement had made was rendered painfully obvious a few years
ago, when a wave of public criticism of accepted values and attitudes arose in Dublin and swept through the country. On television or in university halls one could hear discussions of 'idealism
in Ireland today' which made no mention of the missionaries.
There were even calls for Ireland to 'aid the underdeveloped
countries' as part of a desirable new world-awareness and as if
this would have represented an exciting new venture. One of the
standard things for public pundits to say was that 'we must stop
being inward-looking and become outward-looking'—a statement
which not only the missionaries and the Legionaries of Mary, but
even the postmen delivering letters to the remotest farmhouses
up and down the country, would have found difficult to under-

stand. It was the familiar sacred-secular dichotomy : one small country, but two worlds.

As the old missionary period ends and the mission-sending bodies are faced with the need to overhaul their policy and aims overseas, and their personnel training at home, they are also faced with the need to broaden their base in Irish society, to re-organize and reformulate their appeal to their own people. If the movement which got under way fifty years ago is to go forward with undiminished strength (though necessarily with a new vision and programme), society as a whole and lay professionals will have to play much greater roles in it than hitherto. As for the priests and religious who continue to seek their life's work in Africa and Asia, their motives and purpose will need to be re-formulated in the light of the new view of the Church and of non-Christian religions and cultures which has emerged from Vatican II; new kinds of recruits must be appealed to in new ways. Further, there is need for a sympathetic and cooperative approach to the civic needs and aspirations of the new African and Asian states—for a certain political commitment to them.

A fresh understanding of the situation and its needs, then vision of the desirable goal in the future. When these have been won, there is need for a new language and a new manner of per-suasion to convey the needs to those who can supply them and the vision to those who can implement it. When the new message is ready, a start could be made by the missionary bodies collaborat-ing in the publication of a new, joint journal directed at the in-telligent reading public. The fact that some of them are already exploring together ways and means of doing this is an encourag-ing development.

But all of this is less than half of what the new mission needs. If the Irish society which produces the missionaries (by whatever name) continues to suffer from its inherited socio-cultural dis-orders, from its own anomia, and to accept its crippled condi-tion as a 'normal' way of life, all these new efforts will remain cerebral and merely formal in their scope and effect. The mis-sionary movement needs new people, and these can only come from a new people. Enough harm has been done in Africa and

Asia by modern Europeans naively assuming that they represented the healthy human norm, while in fact they were crippled personalities, spreading a personality virus and a socio-cultural disease.

How this situation might be righted, how Irish society would at least begin to heal itself and gain some experience in this self-therapy before dispatching any further physicians to other peoples, would be another story. But the first step, as in any healing, would be an admission of sickness; the second, a correct diagnosis; the third, a vision of health and a desire for it. For the sake of those Africans, Asians and Latin Americans to whom Irish men and women may some day render a really life-building service in Christ's name, there is a great deal of reflection and analysis, of imagining and desiring, to be done in Ireland, with reference to Irish life, now and in the immediate future.

The following comment on this essay was received from Rev. Brian Gogan, C.S.Sp., a well-known writer on African missionary topics, and published in November 1967:

'Congratulations on your rather complete survey of the twentieth-century missionary movement in Ireland in your July-August issue. You gave an overall view of something which most people only see piecemeal. It was interesting to observe your recognition of the extent to which Irish missionary effort has been committed to more or less humanitarian activity. This is something often overlooked by critics of the Irish approach to the missionary situation when comparing it unfavourably with the more sophisticated methods ascribed to our continental confreres.

'Yet there can indeed be little doubt that educational activity in particular has absorbed mind and energy, to the detriment, no doubt, of other specialized tasks. In illustration of this, one may remark that in 1954 there were more pupils in the elementary schools of one Irish-staffed diocese in West Africa (Owerri, Biafra/ E. Nigeria) than in all the elementary schools in the then French West Africa or Central Africa. (Compare UNESCO, *Current School Enrolment Statistics,* No. 1, 1955, p. 10 with H. Koran, *The Spiritans,* Pittsburgh, 1958, p. 567.)

'Your critique of the movement, on the other hand, is more

difficult either to accept or to reject, since virtually no evidence is advanced in support of its assertions. In view of this, it might interest your readers to see how some of your generalizations stand up in the light of recent mission experience in Biafra/E. Nigeria.

'1. *Insensitivity to citizenship*. It is, I believe, true that Irish missionaries were reserved in their attitudes towards the independence movements in their early stages. But the reasons behind these attitudes were a little more complex than you suggest. Anyone living near the grassroots of African society was acutely aware of the unreal nature of the political structures which colonial powers had imposed on Africa, preserved by force of arms, and to which they were about to blithely entrust the emerging peoples in the name of a wind of change. In point of fact, things have turned out a good deal better than many would have expected, but the pre-independence prospect was not entirely inviting.

'Secondly, independence, when it did come, was warmly welcomed by the missionaries and their essential goodwill was recognized by the politicians as well as by the people.

'Friction which may have arisen was due not to any alienation of either hierarchy or people from the political life of the country but from an inter-church power struggle between Catholics and Protestants, not unlike that in pre-war Holland. Curiously enough, our critics, in this respect, accuse us of being too political. If you were to compare Church-state relationships in those countries largely staffed by Irish missionary personnel with those staffed by other nationalities, I should be inclined to think that the balance would go slightly in favour of the Irish. Education is often the dividing line, yet in Nigeria/Biafra, Sierra Leone, Kenya (and also, I believe, Zambia)—unlike a number of other African states—mission schools have been left under the direction of the Catholic bishops.

'2. *Slowness in the recruitment of clergy*. You mention the slowness of Irish missionaries in recruiting for the priesthood as distinct from recruiting for congregations of religious sisters and brothers. The practical reason behind this fact is that Irish priests tend to look on ordination to the priesthood as an irrevocable step, involving a commitment to something far more sacred than what is promised in religious profession. In spite of our evident failings, most of us try to live it this way. In mission countries we have naturally been slow to invite young men to commit themselves to this step. Slowness, as in mahogany, iroko and oak, can be a virtue. And the actual situation is not so bad as one might be led to believe. About one-fifth of the clergy of Biafra/E. Nigeria come from local dioceses.

'It could be argued, as Fr Adrian Hastings has done (see *African Ecclesiastical Review*, Vol. 8, 1966, No. 3, pp. 146-60, No. 4, pp. 291-8), that the general shortage of African vocations calls for a reappraisal of the whole canonical structure governing the priesthood south of the Sahara. Possibly a ministry more closely related to the norms found in New Testament writings and the Fathers of the Church would be better suited to a Christendom still in gestation. In fact, it is not impossible that the slowness of Irish priests in recruiting to the priesthood may be vindicated even theoretically when we realize to what extent our own forms have been influenced by Cluniac monasticism and counter-reformation asceticism.

'3. *Absence of true love.* You speak of the unhappy impact of missionaries on "peoples whom they have thought they loved but could not—since they never opened their minds to their lives nor sought to know them for their own sakes". This statement comes in a general context which deplores the lack of "systematic, genuinely interested study of the cultures, religions and historical situations of these peoples". There appears to me to be an underlying psychological fallacy in this judgment, which could have unhappy results if allowed to pass unchallenged.

'The assumption seems to be that the knowledge on which valid human relationship is best based, and within which true human love becomes possible, is critical, reflective, systematic—and thereby necessarily conceptual—knowledge. Even to express it in these words is to bring out the weakness of the case. Does a mother need to be fully acquainted with the dynamic theory of early and middle childhood in order to care adequately for her children? Do adults have to form ideologies before they fall in love? What seems to have been overlooked is the role of non-conceptual intellectually conscious awareness of concrete existence, as well as the role of pre-critical conceptual knowledge in forming a real and normal noetic framework for human relationships. These can be illuminated, but also hindered, by science.

'This is not to say that your basic contention is false, that we have neglected to take full account of the cultures in which we work. It is perfectly true, but I would suggest that this lack of mental equipment has been felt more seriously at the level of structure, organization and administration than in day-to-day personal relations. Finally, I might add that as far as I know most Irish missionary communities have already repaired, or are in the process of repairing, this gap in their training. Your encouragement will no doubt help to speed the process.'

12

MAYNOOTH AND THE
UNIVERSITY QUESTION[1]

'This may well be, if not the last, very nearly the last conferring of degrees of the National University of Ireland in Maynooth. The proposal to have one university in Dublin means the end of the National University as it is at present. But there will still be degrees conferred in Maynooth. There is, I believe, general agreement that within the new university framework there will be a place for Maynooth and that it will continue to retain its university status.'

This statement by the then president of Maynooth, Mgr G. Mitchell, at the conferring of degrees at the college in November 1967, reveals the present uncertainty as to the future of Maynooth College. Even the college authorities and the bishops seem unsure as to what that future will be.

Since 1908 Maynooth has been a recognized college of the National University of Ireland in the faculties of arts, philosophy and Celtic studies, and since 1912 in the faculty of science. (The National University has had constituent colleges at Dublin, Cork and Galway.) All Maynooth's seminarians take university courses, but their university life has been lived in isolation at Maynooth with no provision for contact with other undergraduates, or with any lay people except during vacation. Then, from a meeting of the hierarchy on 21 June 1966, the following statement was issued to the press :

'The Second Vatican Council has called for the development of Catholic university facilities, especially in the sphere of philosophy and theology, in order to show the harmony of

[1] January 1968.

162

Christian teaching with true human culture and scientific development, and to provide all priests, religious and laity with the fullest opportunity of Christian formation.

'The Irish bishops at their June meeting have had under consideration how this development could be secured in this country and propose to develop Maynooth as an open centre of higher studies and to extend its facilities and courses so as to meet the requirements, not merely of priests, diocesan and regular, but also of brothers, nuns, and the laity. They have appointed a committee to advise them on the best means of implementing this proposal.'

This statement was welcomed generally as a major breakthrough towards the full utilization of the existing higher education facilities available in the country and as the best basis for clergy-laity dialogue at all levels. But progress since has been disappointing, even allowing for the fact that it will take time fully to implement the bishops' proposals. There has been no vigorous follow-up aimed at attracting and encouraging religious and lay people to enrol, and no sign of the proposed extension of facilities and courses. In the academic year 1966-7, of a total of 577 students, 88 were non-residential 'outsiders'. Of these, 62 were teachers taking a course in the education department, so that they made little contribution to the life of the college. Twelve Society of the Divine Word (SVD) students and one Benedictine nun enrolled in first year theology, and six SVD students in second year theology. Six nuns and one layman enrolled in first year arts and philosophy courses. The complete official silence on the subject since the bishops' statement has led to uncertainty in the minds of the public as to the future of the college.

Meanwhile, in April 1967, the minister for education, Mr Donogh O'Malley, announced that it was no longer reasonable or economic to maintain two separate university establishments in Dublin and that Trinity College (the traditionally Protestant 'Dublin University') and University College, Dublin, (UCD) must merge in a single two-college university. The National University of Ireland would be dissolved, Cork and Galway becoming universities in their own right. The minister did not specify in detail

what form the Dublin merger should take but said he was ready
to listen to suggestions. An inter-college committee was set up
to discuss plans and the academic world was thrown into fer-
ment.

Since University College, Dublin, has roughly three times as
many students, Trinity College understandably fears for its survival as an entity if the merger is complete, while the staff of
UCD seem divided on the issue, the younger members generally
seeming to sympathize with Trinity's wish to preserve its individual tradition. The position of the Cork and Galway colleges
is difficult. With still smaller numbers, how can they hope to survive and attract students in face of the already strong attraction
of the Dublin colleges, and now of the new university which will
dwarf them completely? What is the university framework best
suited to the needs of the country as a whole? Maynooth's position is particularly difficult. Its 500-600 students seem insignificant compared with UCD's 8,000 plus, and as up to now it has
not made any major contribution to the general university life
of the country it tends to be overlooked in the current debate.
The recent appointment of a new president and vice-president,
both young and academically distinguished, may herald a move
by the college and the bishops to rectify this.

Maynooth College was a product of the new Irish Catholic
self-assertion which was beginning to develop towards the end
of the eighteenth century. Irish Catholicism had weathered a
century of suppression, not unmarred, but basically intact. The
first relaxation of the penal laws encouraged a feeling of self-
potential and a belief in the possibility of emancipation in all
fields. The nineteenth century saw a great development of this
self-assertion and, while the fundamental problem was the land
and the respective rights of those who lived off it, education for
Catholics was another basic issue.

The foundation of Maynooth College as a national seminary
was partly intended as a sop to Irish Catholic opinion, bitterly
disappointed in 1795 by the recall of the Lord Lieutenant, Fitz-
william, from whom much in the way of Catholic emancipation
had been hoped. More decisive was the fear, shared by government and bishops, of the effect on the future clergy of Ireland of

the atmosphere of revolutionary France. At the time about four hundred students for the Irish dioceses were being educated at Irish colleges on the Continent, in Rome, Flanders, Spain and Portugal, but the great majority in France and particularly in Paris. The future of these colleges, and access to them, was uncertain also, and government and bishops agreed that it would be safer to educate the students at home where they might learn to be grateful and obedient to the government which subsidized their education. There was a body of opinion, both Catholic and Protestant, in favour of connecting the education of the Catholic clergy in some way with Dublin University, but the bishops submitted that it would be too expensive and 'not appropriate for Catholic priests'.

As it was still illegal to endow 'any college or seminary for the education exclusively for persons professing the Roman Catholic religion', an act of parliament had to be passed to give selected trustees the necessary powers to receive and administer the annual grant of £8,000. The trustees appointed by the government were the four chief Irish law lords (*ex officio* trustees), six Catholic laymen, the four Catholic archbishops, and seven Catholic bishops. As the government left the management of the college in the hands of the trustees, and as neither the *ex officio* nor the lay Catholic trustees interfered to any extent, the bishops had a free hand in organizing and running the college. Maynooth was chosen as a location largely because the Duke of Leinster offered a site there on favourable terms, and the college opened in 1795 with fifty students.

The bishops now had the task of educating the Irish clergy along lines that would satisfy the government as to their loyalty, Rome as to their orthodoxy, and the Irish public as to their sympathy with national aspirations. They made a surprisingly good job of satisfying all three, and particularly in overcoming the initial suspicion among Irish Catholics of the products of a government-subsidized seminary. It was too much to hope also to modify popular Protestant suspicion about what was taught the future priests of Ireland, and during the first sixty years of its existence there were two public inquiries into the condition of the college and its teaching on such subjects as the relative rights of

Church and State, obedience to constituted authority, and the right of the Pope to interfere in temporal affairs.

By 1825 the number of students had increased to over 390 and Maynooth was supplying an average of 50 priests each year to the Irish dioceses, whose total annual need was 80-90. About 260 students for the Irish dioceses were being educated elsewhere, about 120 in diocesan seminaries—the largest number in Carlow and others in Kilkenny, Tuam, Waterford and Wexford —and about 140 on the continent, half of them in Paris. Of the 390 in Maynooth, 250 had free places. So had 20 'senior students' of theology, called Dunboyne students because their department, the Dunboyne, originated with the legacy of the famous Lord Dunboyne, the Catholic bishop of Cork. He succeeded to the title, conformed to the Established Church so that he might marry and produce an heir, but then repented on his deathbed and left a legacy to the college. One of the main purposes of the Dunboyne was the training of future professors and in this it was successful, though one might argue that a greater influx of new blood and ideas would have been valuable.

In 1845, in the teeth of an opposition which included half his own party, Sir Robert Peel increased the annual Maynooth grant to £26,360 on the grounds that it could not do an efficient job if under-financed. A further £30,000 was granted for building and the existing inadequate accommodation was increased by the addition of the Pugin quadrangle—or rather three sides of the quadrangle, as money ran out before it could be completed by the chapel on the fourth side. The McCarthy chapel was added later and paid for by public subscription. The increased grant to Maynooth encouraged the tendency of the smaller diocesan seminaries to send more of their priests abroad all over the English-speaking world. The exodus of the famine years further strengthened this trend.

By 1853 there were 515 students in Maynooth and, of a total of 2,291 diocesan clergy in the country, 1,222 were educated in Maynooth, including two of the four archbishops and 21 of the 25 bishops. There were now twice as many students in Maynooth as were being educated elsewhere for the Irish dioceses. In 1871, after the Irish Church Act of 1869 disestablishing the Church of

Ireland, the annual grant to Maynooth was withdrawn and a lump sum of £369,040 paid instead. Disestablishment did not permanently reduce the number of students. Between 1870 and 1875 they fell by about 100 but quickly recovered and reached 500 again during the eighties. Since 1900 the number of students has remained fairly constant at about 550. The average number of Maynooth ordinations during the present century is 68 per annum and, since the total number of ordinations for the home dioceses is about 90, Maynooth has dominated numerically among the secular clergy of Ireland for at least 120 years.

How far did Maynooth fulfil the hopes of those who founded it? The Protestant archbishop of Dublin, Richard Whately, summed it up from one point of view when he said in 1852 that

'Mr Pitt thought that the young priests were taught disaffection and anti-Anglicanism at Douai, and he created for their education the most disaffected and the most anti-English establishment in Europe.'

This outcome was perhaps not so surprising. Previous to the establishment of Maynooth, the great majority of students for the Irish diocese (some were ordained before they were sent abroad) were educated on the Continent in a distinctly Gallican atmosphere where papal infallibility and the right of the pope to intervene in temporal affairs was denied and obedience to civil authority insisted upon. Now instead of being scattered, isolated groups all over Europe, they were gathered together in one college not fifteen miles from Dublin and where 'no wave of political or social excitement was not, at least to some extent, felt'.

The students were mainly the sons of small farmers and shop-keepers, and therefore closely identified with the land struggle that underlay all Irish history in the nineteenth century. It is true that the first teachers and administrators in the college were themselves products of Continental training, and their influence, implicit if not explicit, was Gallican in tendency. Their interests in the survival of the college strengthened the emphasis on civil obedience, but this may have contributed to stimulate a certain degree of rebelliousness not uncommon among students. Excitement and disturbances in the college coincided with events outside and there were expulsions at the time of the 1798 rising and Emmet's rising in 1803. Any initial lay distrust of the Maynooth priests was disappearing by the 1820s, when they were beginning to predominate among the Irish clergy and formed the backbone of O'Connell's agitation. Their involvement in politics continued to grow and in the 1840s the students were well aware that certain professors sympathized with the Young Irelanders. By this time the staff had grown up in the new tradition and presently it took all Cardinal Cullen's influence to discourage clerical involvement in national politics. The popular picture of the Maynooth priest of the nineteenth century—paternalistic, kindly, not very polished, closely associated with the political and social aspirations of his people, often the local leader and driving force in their effort to attain them—seems generally accurate.

Academically, the college had got off to a good start. Besides being the main reason for the foundation of Maynooth, the French revolution made available refugee scholars from the continent, and the original staff of the college included men, Irish as well as French, who had achieved academic distinction abroad. Delahogue in particular seems to have had a considerable reputation.

The Dunboyne establishment, regarded as the equivalent of a postgraduate school and one in fact when Maynooth became a pontifical university in 1896, was mainly intended to provide teaching staff for the college. This it did from the time the first professors began to retire or die, and Maynooth increasingly provided staff for the diocesan seminaries, so that the theological studies in Ireland soon tended to become inbred and infertile, the more so since financial considerations did not encourage any major policy of sending senior students or staff abroad for further study.

This cut Maynooth off to some extent from intellectual life on the Continent, and made its development lopsided, for during the second half of the century, after the arrival of Cullen from Rome—first as archbishop of Armagh, then as cardinal archbishop of Dublin and papal legate—the strong ultramontane influence was not balanced by direct contact with the philosophical movements especially associated with Germany.

The intellectual tone of the college, still influenced by the Gallican tendency of the original staff, encouraged an attitude of independence towards Rome, while this was balanced by the need to keep Rome assured of the college's orthodoxy. On the other hand, the close identification of the students—and the second and succeeding generations of professors—with Irish politico-social problems encouraged an independent attitude towards the government. The parish clergy synthesized these influences into the well-known attitude 'religion from Rome but politics from home'. In these circumstances it is not surprising to find that there was an emphasis on intellectual moderation, with no innovation in theology. Maynooth's best-known theological writer in the nineteenth century, Patrick Murray, was very much in the ultramontane, defence-of-the-faith, school. Original thinking or speculation which might attract unwelcome notoriety was not encouraged.

The connection between staff and hierarchy was, and remains, a further complicating factor. It has been noted that, from the foundation of the college, those bishops who were trustees had the controlling influence on the college. Since the disestablishment of the Church of Ireland the bishops have been confirmed in complete authority. The present trustees are the four archbishops and thirteen bishops and the entire hierarchy are associated with them in control of the college. This means that the academic staff have had no direct voice in college policy. Again, Maynooth was, and is, the major source of Irish bishops. During the first hundred years of the college's existence a Maynooth professor became a bishop on average once every four years.

This had, and has, two effects. First, it disrupts the continuity of tenure and staff that would encourage the emergence of a specifically 'Maynooth' theology, at the same time constituting a serious brain-drain. Second, it militates against wholehearted acceptance by the professorial staff of the academic approach to theology. The approach to theology of an episcopal candidate must differ from that of an academic theologian. In Maynooth the lines seem sometimes to have got confused.

The attitude of staff and bishops to the controversial Professor Walter McDonald illustrates some of these complications. He was not allowed to publish his theological writings, more because the bishops were afraid of adverse publicity than because they were seriously worried by his opinions. He was left undisturbed in his long tenure of the prefectship of Dunboyne (1882-1920), a potent formative influence all those years on the only postgraduate students of Catholic theology in Ireland.

McDonald was an academic with no ambition to be a bishop and his assessment of Maynooth is interesting. He felt that the teaching was out of touch with the philosophical and theological issues of the day. As a student he never heard of the principle of development as applied to theology. The nineteenth-century rationalist approach to biblical sources was not discussed and,

> 'while we were not in the least danger of joining the Anglican or the Irish Protestant Church, some of us were painfully disturbed when we could no longer keep our eyes closed to the arguments of the rationalists.'

As to the products of the Maynooth teaching, McDonald thought that the aim was to produce

> 'good average men. The worst of it is that we succeed; for, while our average man is very good, our best men are poor—as compared, that is, with those who are trained elsewhere.'

This judgment probably had a good deal of truth in it.

Nineteenth-century Maynooth was very much the product of its environment and of current politico-social problems and it could claim to have satisfied the needs of the community fairly well. As the century drew to a close the environment and its needs were changing, and there were men in Maynooth who felt that Maynooth must move with the times and try to satisfy the new needs. Home rule in some form or other was becoming inevitable and the question of university education for Catholics was now acute.

There had been a number of attempts to solve this problem. Peel's non-denominational Queen's Colleges of 1845 had failed because the bishops finally rejected them. Catholic lay opinion generally was for accepting them and the bishops were evenly

divided for and against until the arrival in Ireland of Archbishop
Cullen finally turned the balance against mixed education. The
bishops' veto on Catholic attendance at these colleges, while not
entirely effective, did prevent them from solving the problem.
The Catholic University, founded in 1854 with John Henry Newman as rector, was no solution either because it had no state endowment and the Catholic public was not enthusiastic enough to
support it adequately.

After various abortive proposals, the Royal University was
established in 1879 as an examining body only, but endowed to
grant prizes and fellowships and thus channel some of the public
funds to Catholic institutions. Maynooth was enthusiastic at first,
then withdrew its students because it felt that the examination
system was weighted against them. Later this decision was re-
gretted and all students were required to take the university examinations. The Royal University was so far from being a final
solution that two royal commissions investigated the situation in
the first years of the twentieth century, the Robertson Commission and the Fry Commission. Neither could find a solution to
reconcile all the interested parties, but it is interesting to note that
the Fry Commission, in a majority report, opposed the establishment of two teaching universities in Dublin, and recommended
enlarging Dublin University to include five colleges: Trinity,
University College (the former Catholic University) and the three
Queen's Colleges in Belfast, Cork and Galway. This proved un-
acceptable due to diehard anti-Catholic opinion and also in part
to the Catholic bishops, who by now felt a strong ultramontane
suspicion of all non-denominational education.

At this time a body of opinion among the staff of Trinity
College favoured coming to terms with the Catholics, but enthusiasm on the part of the bishops would have been necessary
for anything to come of it. Finally the Irish Universities Act of
1908 dissolved the Royal University and set up two new universities, Queen's University in Belfast and the National University
of Ireland, comprising UCD and the former Cork and Galway
Queen's Colleges. This compromise gave state endowment to
what was in effect Catholic education, but at the price of excluding any endowment for theology. Maynooth was affiliated as a

recognized college with no endowment. This very make-shift solution has remained the framework of Irish university education ever since.

The biggest direct influence from Ireland during the nineteenth century on the Catholic Church elsewhere in the English-speaking world was, on the one hand, the steady stream of priests from the diocesan seminaries, many of whom later became bishops abroad and, on the other hand, those bishops who had been trained in Maynooth. During the first century of the college's existence fifteen Maynooth men became bishops in the USA, Canada, Australia and South Africa. For these bishops and priests and the churches they helped to develop, Maynooth was the effective centre of Catholic teaching right into the twentieth century, though today both Maynooth and the Irish Church have lost this position of leadership. The formation which Maynooth had evolved, in answer to Irish conditions, for Irish priests, was well enough adapted to the nineteenth-century surroundings of the Catholic Church in English-speaking countries where the Church, like that at home, was emerging from a period of oppression and establishing its rights to freedom in a Victorian, liberal democratic environment.

But the kind of Catholicism which these Irishmen helped to build was too defensive and inward-looking to adapt readily to the pluralist, secularist society that has developed generally throughout the other countries of the English-speaking world today, and became obviously out-of-date there sooner than in Ireland.

The future of Maynooth has to be considered from two points of view : first, from that of the primary purpose of the college, the education of priests for pastoral work in Ireland; second, from that of its potential contribution to the university system of the country. There is a growing body of opinion, both within and without the college, that these points of view are not irreconcilable.

As to priestly formation the Vatican II decree states :

'Before seminarians commence their specifically ecclesiastical studies, they should already have received that literary and scientific education which is a prerequisite to higher studies in their own countries.'

The decree also required that dogmatic theology be taught in its historical sequence, as an evolving science. It states further that,

'with due regard to the conditions of different countries, students should be introduced to a fuller understanding of the churches and ecclesial communities separated from the Holy See, so that they may be able to take part in promoting the restoration of unity among all Christians according to the decision of the Council.'

These three recommendations will be fulfilled more easily in a university setting than in an isolated seminary and, simply from the point of view of the better education of priests for Irish dioceses, many feel that Maynooth's connection with the National University should become a real integration into the new university framework.

From the university point of view it needs to be remembered that the present lack of a school of theology in the National University is an accident of circumstances and was not decided on in principle. In 1908 the only way to subsidize university education for Irish Catholics from public funds was to leave out theology, and that is why it was done. Today the circumstances which made the university question virtually insoluble for over a hundred years have changed and it is possible to approach university planning with the avowed object of best serving the needs of the community. People widely accept today that theology can only develop properly in a university setting. It is increasingly seen as a developing science, an evolving and on-going investigation and clarification of the revealed truths of Christianity, which for its proper growth needs contact with the other disciplines of the university, thus keeping the theologian in touch both with the constant advances in the physical, biological and behavioural sciences and with the principal source of the intellectual life of his own civil community. Isolated in a clerical seminary, theologians can easily fail to become aware of the really relevant questions and thus fail to face them—or even attempt to answer them.

It is well to recall that similar views as to the need of a university setting for Irish theology were put forward by Maynooth men during the early years of this century. The bishop of Clonfert, Dr Thomas O'Dea, a former professor and vice-president of the college, published a pamphlet in 1903 giving suggestions already proposed in evidence before the Robertson Commission. He suggested that Maynooth be included in whatever university scheme was adopted for Catholics, and that the Dunboyne be transferred to a divinity school in Dublin with a house of residence for the postgraduate students of theology from Maynooth and for postgraduate art students. He thought it necessary for the clergy to take part in the university life of the nation, and envisaged close cooperation between the arts and theology schools in Dublin and Maynooth respectively. This transference of the Dunboyne was also suggested in 1907 by the theology faculty in Maynooth. Walter McDonald summed it all up when he said that it was 'lamentable' that

> 'our greatest school of theology should be cut away so much from the influence of the currents of thought that are shaping the minds of those who will soon be our educated laity. Theology is a synthesis of the sciences. But how is one to synthesize who does not know the elements and how is one to know the sciences who is out of living touch with them?'

On the other hand, the university needs theology as much as theology needs the university. Sixty years ago it might have been possible to hope that a university without theology could be useful and successful, but today there is a new awareness of the interdependence of the various disciplines, if only because it is recognized that no man can be a master of them all and yet that if he ignores the findings and questionings of others, he does so at the expense of his own discipline. In our culture the university is the centre of intellectual life, and if theological discussion there is at an amateur level in contrast to a professional level in other disciplines, there is an imbalance which does no good to any of the studies involved. Basically, experience has shown that theology is too much at the heart of things, too much 'a synthesis of the sciences', to be ignored.

Trinity College has an Anglican divinity school. Whatever the final structure of the new Dublin University it is certain that Catholic theology will have to be included. This can be done in a single open school of theology with Catholic and Protestant staff or in separate though cooperating schools of theology. There is general agreement that Maynooth's special strength as a theological centre would need to be exploited by having it recognized as the focus of Catholic theology in the new university. Maynooth has been a pontifical university since 1896, is the largest degree-giving school of Catholic theology in the country, has the only post-graduate school, and publishes an internationally-known theological journal, *The Irish Theological Quarterly*.

The way seems open to do what was not found possible in 1908, to integrate Maynooth fully with the university of Dublin —the campus will be well scattered anyhow—make her school of theology the nucleus and centre of Catholic theology in the university, and set up a department of theology in Dublin in close cooperation with Maynooth.

This could be staffed in the beginning from Maynooth and from the other seminaries and religious houses that had talent to contribute but whose numerical resources were slighter. It would offer courses in theology for degrees combining theology with other subjects and for a full theology degree. It would be expected and hoped that, as this degree was taken by lay people, lay representation in the faculty would follow. This should be one of the main objects. Unless lay people get involved in theology at the professional level, their views cannot make much impression on the clerical theologians and any genuine dialogue remains difficult, if not impossible.

As for Maynooth College itself, theology there would have to be put in a genuine university setting. Experience from other countries suggests that this would require building up the enrolment to at least two thousand students. This number of students—at least two-thirds of them lay men and women— would be sufficient for a vigorous liberal-arts college in undergraduate courses of the type proven valuable in the United

States to relieve pressure on over-large universities—which, it is being found by experience, cannot give students a satisfactory university environment. The distance between Dublin and Maynooth means much less today than it did sixty years ago and it should be possible for the two to complement rather than exactly parallel each other.

It has been suggested that Cork and Galway should each develop an academic speciality which would both give to each college a special character of its own and contribute to the overall university resources of the country. This might be a fruitful suggestion for Maynooth also, and one possibility that has been canvassed is a school of Afro-Asian studies which would draw into the stream of Irish intellectual life the major visible achievement of Irish Catholicism in the twentieth century, the missionary movement. So far this movement has remained completely outside the mainstream of intellectual life, neither contributing to it nor receiving from it anything of value. A school of Afro-Asian studies, teaching cultural studies, languages, anthropology, ethnology and missiology would, apart from its contribution to learning, be of immediate and long-term benefit to the missionary bodies, while enabling them to make their contribution to the intellectual life of the country. It could also become a focal point for cultural contacts with Africa and Asia and for aid projects in the underdeveloped countries.

The decision of the minister for education that there is to be a merger in Dublin and a reorganization generally, along with his request to the parties concerned to submit suggestions, has given an opportunity for discussion and planning that may not come again. Now, for the first time in the modern history of higher education in Ireland, the discussion is free to concern itself solely with the best interests of the nation and the Church. It is obvious that Maynooth has a contribution to make, and something to gain itself by seizing the opportunity to integrate fully into the intellectual life of the country. Positive suggestions must now be made and the details hammered out in discussions open to all interested parties. So far, however, since the original statement of June 1966, there has been no statement of interest by Maynooth, or rather, on its behalf by the bishops—for under the present constitution of the college it is they, not the academic body itself, who are competent to make such a statement. As far as the public is aware, the bishops have not made positive overtures to the other colleges.

There will of course be problems in integration, if it happens, a major one being the bishops' authority in a school of theology in Dublin; but it will not be possible to solve them unless, to begin with, some definite proposals are produced, if only as a basis for discussion. The relationship of seminaries and clerical training to universities is being discussed openly all over the Christian world. The findings in other countries may help, though the solution must ultimately depend on what is found best suited to Irish conditions. Unless the discussion starts soon the opportunity may pass. So far the Irish Catholic laity have displayed little public interest in the future of their national seminary and pontifical university, which has played such an outstanding part in modern Irish history. That this should be so among a laity where the formal obligations of membership of the Church are almost universally honoured might well cause concern to the hierarchy and lead them to question the wisdom of continuing to rely on the present institutional structures of the Church.

13

HOW IRISH IS IRISH CATHOLICISM?

Television discussions and interviews have played an outstanding part in making the Irish public aware of the Second Vatican Council and of the new thinking generally in the Roman Catholic Church. Probably in no other country except Holland did the aggiornamento movement hit the television screens with quite the same impact.

The discussion which we reproduce here in shortened form, and by kind permission of Radio Telefís Éireann, was broadcast from the Dublin studios on 15 January 1967. The discussion was chaired by Seán Mac Réamoinn, a radio and television journalist who attended all four sessions of the Council and has been one of the leading evangelists of Church renewal in Ireland. Taking part in the discussion were, in order of speaking: Desmond Fennell, editor of Herder Correspondence; *Fr Thomas Mc-Inerney, O.P., who has followed courses in television in Rome and New York and is now professor of fundamental theology at a Dominican house of studies near Dublin; and Kevin B. Nowlan, associate professor of modern history (nineteenth century) at University College, Dublin.*

Before the discussion began some of the better-known religious images from a typical Catholic repository—St Jude, the Little Flower, the Child of Prague, the Sacred Heart, etc. were shown on the screen.

MAC REAMOINN : Now, you saw there at the beginning of the programme a number of pictures which perhaps an outside observer or non-believer might regard as the household garment of Ireland. Certainly not Irish in their provenance any of them,

they form part of the Irish devotional scene. How Irish is Irish
Catholicism at home and abroad? In the November issue of
Herder Correspondence there was an article called 'The Myth
of the Irish : A Failure of American Catholic Scholarship'. Now
this article, which talks about Irish Catholicism, and the attitude
to it among American Catholic scholars today, is perhaps a con-
venient jumping-off ground for our discussion. Look, Desmond,
would you like to say a word about this article?

FENNELL : Yes, I'll say a word about it, but to get away from it
quickly. The article dealt with the discussion of Irish Catholicism
that has been going on among American Catholics over the past
few years and criticized some insular and almost racial ideas
which had crept into that discussion. But what we want to talk
about tonight is how we, ourselves, have fallen into the same
errors in the debate about, and public criticism of, Irish Catholicism which has been going on for the past few years in Ireland.
We have been finding lots of things wrong, and rightly so, but
we haven't really been getting at the root of what is wrong because we have been seeing far too many things that are part of
the cultural history of Western Europe or part of the Church in
all of Western Europe—we have been seeing these things as
specifically Irish. For instance, we have been complaining that
various devotions of minor importance have pushed Christ and
the Mass to one side. Now, of course, they are complaining about
this in every country in Western Europe at the moment and, in
fact, these devotions which have taken the place of the eucharist
or of the Mass are mostly of French and Italian and, in general,
Continental origin. They did not arise in this country. We have
complained about the tastelessness of many of the devotional
objects in our churches. Again these are of Italian, Belgian and
French origin, not a specifically Irish problem. We have complained about our squeamishness in relation to sexual things,
about our idea that sin is almost equivalent to sexual sin but, of
course, these have been prevalent in every country in Europe,
in the Protestant cultures and the Catholic cultures in the nineteenth and twentieth centuries, and to an extreme degree in the
English-speaking world. After all, our modern Catholicism was
formed in an era we call Victorian. Briefly, I throw open for

discussion the thesis, the statement, that what we call Irish Catholicism is simply the fusion of nineteenth-century Victorian culture with the thing that came from Rome to this country in the nineteenth century, the thing that came from the Continent. That's all we have, that's what we call Irish Catholicism.

MAC REAMOINN : Now, this is something we can take as a basis for discussion. First of all, perhaps, to clear up a couple of what I regard as common vulgar notions about this subject, and I am sure we are in agreement that they don't hold water for a moment : one is the Jansenist myth, the notion that because when Maynooth was founded some of the first members of the faculty there had been educated abroad, therefore in some mysterious way they brought the Jansenist heresy with them. I take it we would agree that this doesn't hold water at all. Then there is the sort of person who says to you, 'Look, I am not an Irish Catholic, I am a Roman Catholic.' You could argue that there is no substance in what he thinks he is saying.

MCINERNEY : Is Irish Catholicism specific, is it distinct from any other form of national Catholicism? I would say yes, and I think the main mark of distinction is that it is a rather negative type of Catholicism in this sense, that it has no positively specific marks which you could point to as being definitely Irish. We think of the French church as being a highly intellectual church, we think of the German church as being, at the moment anyway, a liturgical church, we think of the Irish church as being a practising church. A practising church is . . . *(interruptions)* . . . thinking in the terms which are generally current now, a practising church is a negative virtue almost. The Irish church as a practising church is primarily a pragmatic church interested in the salvation of its people, and the motivation behind any changes, which are very necessary in certain parts in the Church in Ireland, will have to be this idea of the salvation of the people.

MAC REAMOINN : Dr Nowlan, would you like to take up Desmond Fennell's remark now, that what we have today comes from what we got in post-Emancipation days?

NOWLAN : I would go a very long way with both the previous speakers in their analysis of the situation. Of course, the nineteenth century was enormously important in the shaping of

modern Irish Catholicism. You have just to look at the vast number of churches and convents and monasteries that were built in
the nineteenth century—for good or evil—in a particular archi-
tectural style and so on. But I would go, I think, a stage further
and say that Irish Catholicism has certain distinctive features,
historical features if you like—one was that Irish Catholics were,
in a sense, a minority; although a majority in this island, they
were a minority within the area governed by the English from the
Reformation onwards. This was a fact, particularly after the
breakdown in the seventeenth century of the old Gaelic order,
they hadn't even a political structure within which to express
themselves. Now this produced a number of difficulties and problems. You couldn't have the same external sort of Catholicism,
for good or evil, that you had in other countries. Secondly, because of the disappearance of a Catholic aristocracy, the priests
took a role, which they also did in Slovakia, of becoming the
spokesmen of the people almost of necessity, both in political and
in other terms, and therefore were very closely identified with the
people, and I believe this is very important in understanding the
nature of Irish Catholicism. And thirdly, in the nineteenth century—this is where I agree very much with Desmond Fennell—
in the nineteenth century the Irish Catholic Church, straight from
the time of Daniel O'Connell onwards, had to come to terms with
the problem of how can it live in an essentially Protestant world.
It evolved the very interesting thing of a Catholic liberalism, of
a 'free Church in a free State', to quote Cavour out of context,
and I think we have inherited it. In our modern context I believe
the most fruitful thing to have is this inheritance of freedom, of
a lack of a link between Church and State. This, I think, is something terribly important for the fruitful development of our
modern Catholicism.

MAC REAMOINN : Thank you, and I think Desmond has a word to
say on this.

FENNELL : Yes, I would sum up what you are saying, whether
you accept it or not, Kevin, as that in the nineteenth century our
real achievement was to produce a Catholic version of Anglo-
Saxon culture. In other words, we had its liberalism, its
democracy, its separation of Church and State—inasmuch as this

separation was part of the Liberal and American aspects of Anglo-Saxon culture. We had its philistinism, its puritanism, its anti-intellectualism, everything.

MAC REAMOINN : I would like to discuss this point of the free church in the free society. Now, without wishing on the past notions that are particularly ours, I think that there is a certain basis for the argument that the notion of a separation between the religious and civil powers was one which in Ireland long pre-dated the nineteenth-century situation, that the mere fact, for instance, that Henry II came to Ireland armed with a papal bull made Irish Christians very suspicious of any notion of a close link between Church and State ... *(interruptions)*.

NOWLAN : I think, Seán, with all due respect, that you are project-ing modern notions back into a world where our concept of Church and State and the relations between Church and State didn't exist.

MAC REAMOINN : Surely in the Middle Ages there were many examples of the Irish constantly making this distinction.

NOWLAN : Well, no, because of the extraordinary relationship be-tween the man who was head of the *tuath* and the man who was bishop or abbot of the predominant monastery in the area. The whole problem of the *éireannach* in fact comes in here.

FENNELL : Kevin, I would like to ask you, would you accept that the main area of our creativity as Catholics inside the universal Church in the last hundred and fifty years has been political?

NOWLAN : Very largely. Because of the curious role we played in the English-speaking world in the post-Famine era, Irish Catholicism of course takes on a role perhaps it doesn't deserve otherwise, in the sense that this essentially pious, practical—as distinct from intellectual—Catholicism is exported all over the English-speaking world, and has, as you know, made its impact, again for good or evil, on the structure of modern world Catho-licism.

MCINERNEY : Actually, this whole discussion bears out a point I would like to make. What makes Irish Catholicism specific, which is our problem tonight, is this—that all our Catholic problems are ones with regard to organization and with regard to politics, social situation and everything else. Rarely in Irish Catholic society is there ever a problematic on the level of faith, on the level of salvation. The specific of Irish Catholicism is that we almost naturalize our faith, which happens to be a gift of God. We take it for granted.

MAC REAMOINN : It is, perhaps, not without significance that, in the Irish language, if you want to translate 'religion' you normally use the word *creideamh*.

MCINERNEY : Yes, belief. . . . We seem to take it for granted. In fact if you are looking for a specific contribution of the Irish Church to the Church we know today, it's in the field of the penitential, where private confession became the practice and where one had to make quick judgments and one ladled out penances for various sins. What specifies Irish Catholicism for me, at the moment, is this, that the problems are very often moral problems and never problems with regard to faith, with regard to belief. This has always been the Irish tradition, and it may go back to our native language indeed, because I believe that somebody once claimed that in the Irish language there are two words to distinguish the idea of being : one as the 'act' to be, and the other as present reality. Now, to me, that immediately indicates that Irish is not a metaphysical language, which means that we quantify things which are living, and we seem to quantify our religion to a great degree on this level of moral problematic. What can I do to be a good Catholic, how far can I go either way?

MAC REAMOINN : I do think, Father, that that is a bit of romantic nonsense. The *is/tá* distinction is found in Spanish, it's found in Latin—

(Fr McInerney attempts to come back into discussion . . . interruptions.)

NOWLAN : I think this is why the *Herder Correspondence* article is particularly important. I think that two forms of modern Catholicism which are strikingly similar are American and Irish. For the same reason I go a long way with this influence of nineteenth-century evangelicism—I think it had a very big impact on both countries . . . it's a terribly important factor.

MCINERNEY : If I may say so, Irish Catholicism as now practised

in America is already outdated in Ireland—it is the Irish Catholicism of the early nineteen hundreds. . . .

NOWLAN : Oh, that is very true, very true.

MAC REAMOINN : Perhaps some of us would say that the Catholicism of the penal crosses is something we might take another
hard look at, that we might find in that kind of spirituality something far closer to the needs of today than in that of the nineteenth century.

MCINERNEY : I would think that. What strikes me is that much of
the form of Irish Catholicism, from the point of view of
devotional objects and that, is a soft form, a nineteenth-century
form in fact, and that the penal crosses and the old Irish prayers
indicate a more robust form of belief.

FENNELL : A more intellectual form. . . .

MCINERNEY : Intellectual indeed, but perhaps not cerebrally so,
intuitionally so, and the very debates that are going on at the
moment in Ireland with regard to, say, the clergy/laity relation,
the urgency that people seem to have to know where church
monies and the rest are going, would indicate to me a return to
this strong form of belief which is indicated by the penal crosses
and so on.

NOWLAN : I think you are idealizing it a wee bit, Father.

FENNELL : But even on the most pragmatic of levels, surely what
makes a culture or a religion Irish or German or French is the
inheritance of a continuous heritage of hundreds and hundreds
of years of a particular form of that religion or culture in the one
country; and certainly any Irish Catholic who goes to the Continent finds out that he belongs to an extremely rootless Catholic
life. He goes to Germany or he goes to Spain or he goes to the
Tyrol and he finds people still celebrating the saints of their forefathers, indeed praying much more to Irish saints, as I have
noticed myself in central Europe, than they do in Ireland.

MAC REAMOINN : Would any of you, by the way, like to look at
this point? Is it possible to argue that the integrity of the specifically Irish Christian tradition was maintained by the people rather
than by the priests?

MCINERNEY : The big problem is that we don't know what the
specifically Irish tradition was.

MAC REAMOINN : Well, I think, Father, that there are some evidences of this in pilgrimage, in prayer, in the practices of the people which were, at times, even frowned upon by the clergy.

MCINERNEY : This should surely have influenced the form of Catholicism, say in the nineteenth century. I would take some issue with both of you, if I may, a little bit. You mentioned Germany and Spain and the residual culture and the rest of it; I find that the Irish Catholic is at home in what I would term St Sulpice Christianity. We are close to this continental Catholicism in the tradition of St Sulpice . . . *(interruptions)* . . . alienated from our own traditions.

MAC REAMOINN : A lot of things have remained, but you see there was also in fact the destruction of a culture in the nineteenth century. And this is surely relevant to our question. I mean, how far it is relevant we could argue about all night. I think it is interesting, for instance, to read the pastorals, say, of Archbishop McIntyre in Dublin in the eighteenth century and to trace the quality of the Catholic life of that time, living on sufferance, gradually emerging, and then to see how it took its toys, its decorations as it were. . . .

NOWLAN : But Seán, aren't we being a bit hard. Here they were in a completely Protestant ascendancy world. They were going to show they were as good, if not better. . . .

MAC REAMOINN : One is not criticizing, one is only saying. . . .

MCINERNEY : This brings us to the fundamental question with regard to Irish Catholicism. Why could we lose a culture and retain our faith, when so often people say that the faith is carried by the culture. Because, I think, in the Irish tradition we have always had this curious belief that the faith is something given.

(The discussion is brought to an end:)

MAC REAMOINN : How Irish is it? This is something we obviously won't resolve tonight, gentlemen. Thank you for your very valuable contributions. I think that anything that we could say about this at the moment can only be the beginning of a debate which is of great importance for the future of Christians in Ireland and, because we are a missionary country, abroad.

POSTSCRIPT: THE MIND OF
CATHOLIC IRELAND

First some recent developments and non-developments. The decision to merge the two Dublin university colleges was only one of the educational events in 1967. Free post-primary schooling, for all except boarding-school pupils, was introduced in the Republic, the state bearing the cost. Since this means that the religious and priests, who run most of the post-primary schools, are now precluded from charging fees, their schools have become directly dependent on the public purse. At the same time, schools curricula and the examinations system have been subjected to critical review and revision. In the North, a government measure offering increased grants to Catholic voluntary schools in return for increased control by local authorities has met with opposition from the bishops, on the grounds that the local authorities, which are Protestant-controlled, have not been distinguished for fair dealing towards Catholics.

In July 1967 a new censorship law in the Republic undid the massive bannings of contemporary novels which had occurred largely in the thirties and forties. All books banned before July 1955 were unbanned and a twelve year limit set on future bannings, except in the case of books advocating artificial contraception or abortion. Towards the end of the year an informal inter-party committee on constitutional reform presented an interim report. It recommended, among others things, that the clauses recognizing the 'special position' of the Catholic Church and giving express recognition to other religious bodies be removed from the Constitution; further, that the clause prohibiting legislation for divorce be removed and another clause substituted allowing for divorce legislation to cover cases where divorce was not contrary to the religious tenets of the persons concerned. Both

186

recommendations would, of course, require a referendum vote to become effective. Cardinal Conway, Archbishop of Armagh, and both archbishops of the Church of Ireland made statements rejecting divorce on behalf of their churches. Leaders of other Protestant denominations welcomed the committee's recommendation on the subject.

After a relative recession during 1966, the Republic's economy made a strong recovery, once more achieving an annual growth rate of 4%. Emigration fell to approximately 15,000, thus continuing its general decline in recent years from the figure of 54,000 for 1958. The marriage rate in the younger age groups maintained the sharp rise which took place during the fifties and early sixties. The Irish application for entry to the European Common Market made no real progress. In Cyprus and the Middle East the Army continued its work on behalf of the United Nations. For the first time, a group of foreign cadets—from Zambia—came for training in the Irish Cadet School.

An Association of the Religious Press and a Catechetical Association joined the other associations which have arisen since the Council. The debate about 'the state of the Church', which was so vigorous during the Council years, no longer provides headlines. The bishops' Council policy is concentrating on reform of seminary training and curricula and on reform of religious instruction in the schools. Liturgical change has varied in degree from diocese to diocese, Dublin representing a conservative extreme.

No effective steps have been taken to revitalize the Catholic people through the creation of consultative institutions. Unlike a section of the Dutch Catholic laity, Irish lay Catholics in the present century have not been very interested in theological matters. The metaphysics of republicanism and of the Gaelic cultural movement have absorbed a lot of the mental energy which went into theology in Holland. Since the Council, various devotions have declined in popularity. Confraternities and the Legion of Mary are finding it increasingly difficult to recruit members. At the same time, there has been a considerable growth of Christian social works of various kinds.

With a sharp rise in the number of drop-outs from seminary

studies, there has been some concern about the vocations situation : the bishops have appointed a commission of sociologists to investigate. But there has been no movement out of the ranks of the priesthood. The *rapport* which got under way in the fifties between the clergy and artists in paint, metal, stone, glass and wood has continued to develop. Modern-style churches have become fairly commonplace. But no *rapport* has yet been established with the literary or musical artists, and since literature and music are the typical forms of artistic expression in Ireland, this is a serious lack.

The reports I have brought together in this book were written largely for a readership outside Ireland. The principal purpose of the book is to give news of Irish Catholicism in the twentieth century, and more particularly in the 1960s, to interested readers abroad. But news well given is explanation as well : this composite report is also an attempt to explain some aspects of recent Irish history. In this respect, I believe it can contribute to Irish Catholic self-understanding.

What these pages offer under this heading is not so much 'the facts'—many of which are more or less known to Catholics in Ireland—as an explanatory view of Irish Catholic life today which comes closer to the reality and is more intelligible in depth than any of the explanatory views of themselves which Irish Catholics lived with up to a few years ago. The trouble with those earlier views was a very fundamental one : they did not fulfil the necessary conditions of explanation.

Explanation of anything in particular requires, first of all, that we recognize the *kind of thing* it is. If it belongs to a category of reality which we know well, and if we proceed to relate it, in our explanation, to that category, we are laying the basis of an explanatory view that will be coherent, intelligible in depth and useful. If the phenomenon to be explained is a people's life, the category of reality which we most need to know, and to which we must primarily relate that life, is *man alive*—the human condition, man as he is and has been in his history on this earth. However, since the life of a people takes place within a particular cultural and historical context, it must be realated to this category of reality too, to its *particular cultural and historical context.*

Explanation further requires *analysis* into parts or elements and the consideration of these singly and in relation to each other. But the final, constantly recurring aim must remain *a view of the whole*, with all the constituent elements understood in the context of this whole view. Since no element of a people's life has any reality on its own, neither has it any meaning for us if seen in isolation.

By offering, in a necessarily sketchy and tentative way, *an analytical, related view of Catholic Irish life seen whole and as a human reality*, this book provides something which has hitherto not been available in Ireland. If this is not immediately clear, it will be clearer when we have examined the mind of Catholic Ireland, and its way of seeing Irish reality, over the past century or so. (At present, our self-understanding is in a state of confusion and transition, there is no over-riding agreement as to what we are or how it is with us.)

At least since the nineteenth century we have had no comprehensive and intelligible language of description for our lives as actually lived, and hence no comprehensive framework of analysis such as would have accompanied that kind of language. There was no manner of narrating and describing which sought to reflect and render intelligible the overall actuality of Irish Catholic life as a human and contemporary phenomenon. This was because we had lost sight of the unity and internal relatedness of human life as such, and thus of the human condition as it actually is and of our own humanity as it actually was and is. Though an abstraction labelled *man* remained behind, and though we squeezed it as a secondary, accidental kind of thing into the national, religious and racial categories which we had come to consider primary, *man as he is in his life on earth* had disappeared from our view of ourselves, taking the world with him.

True, during the seminal period of the revolution, from the foundation of the Gaelic League in 1893 up to 1918, revolutionary humanists, by their lives and their writings, made a bid to reinstate man in his Irish context and to relate that context to man. Modern Irish literature, from Joyce, Yeats and Corkery onwards, has provided glimpses of Irish Catholic realities seen as human realities—as world realities. But these essays in integrated, humanized vision were not availed of or developed in those sectors of society where our collective self-understanding, such as it was, continued to be determined.

Instead we were forced to view ourselves through two categories, 'Irish' and 'Catholic' (or 'Ireland' and 'Church'), which *in our understanding of them* defied analysis in general human terms, and through a series of unrelated abstractions from our actual life. Leaving 'Irish' and 'Catholic' for later treatment, I shall look at the unrelated abstractions now. There was 'church history' and there was 'history' proper (meaning largely political and military history); there were the 'religious', the 'secular' and the 'political' spheres, there were 'morality' and 'culture'. For each of these, and for other similarly abstracted elements of our life, there was a special kind of language and a corresponding analysis, and those languages and analyses were not related to each other.

As a result, there was no view available of Irish Catholic life as it was, though this was not realized. Naturally, people wanted and needed to know things and to say things about themselves as members of the group that defined them and about the life they shared together. So they looked at one or other of the abstracted elements—or at combinations of them—linked them somehow with 'Irishness' or 'Catholicism' or with both together, and imagined that they were looking at and talking about themselves. Statements about 'the Irish', 'life in Ireland', 'Irish Catholicism', 'the Church' and 'Ireland' were not lacking. But they bore no direct relationship to reality. Their degree of insight was that of newspapers, old-style catechisms, nationalist rhetoric, positivistic learning, public-house eloquence and adolescents' dreams.

This blindness to ourselves was common to all, but its continuance must be laid squarely at the door of our learned academics : it was no accident that the most profound and comprehensive view of us published in English in the last forty years—Seán de Fréine's *The Great Silence*—was not the work of a professor or even of a graduate. Whether located in theological seminaries or in institutions actually called 'universities', the University as such failed to fulfil its fundamental role as the ordinary source of general light and comprehensive vision. Expert about many individual trees, and about groups of trees, the professors were blind to the wood and failed to show it to us. Disdaining 'generalization' and making it sound like a dirty word, trained to pick holes in the generalizations of others, they failed to use their learning and insights to supply serviceable generalizations of their own. Poets, saints and heroes are the definitive generalizers, but they can fulfil this role only where there is already a skeleton of well-founded communal vision crying out to them for flesh and blood. Lacking this, they wither and limp—and we wither and limp with them.

But men live by generalization, needing it for their minds and souls and actions as their bodies need food. Into the vacuum left by the University—by this *trahison des clercs*—the shoddy, enslaving generalizations poured : from press, mass media and advertising, from power-seekers, demagogues and alienators of every kind. We lived by these for lack of better, but 'live' is hardly the word. Seeing no further than the ends of our noses, we were led by our noses, our banality of vision making our lives banal. By their very nature, these vulgar generalizers and generalizing agencies pursue aims antagonistic to our need for an adequate general view. Our confusion is not their worry, but their advantage. For reasons inherent in their nature and their aims, they employ the terms of reference of our self-understanding—the fragmented ones and such words as *Irish, Catholic, Ireland, Christian, Church*—both carelessly and in whatever way best suits their political, commercial or ideological interests. We, lacking an adequate general view—cut off from reality as in a Chinese prison—lack also the defensive criteria which such a view provides.

Clearly, the fragmentation of vision and the thraldom to abstraction which I have described above were Irish variants of a modern European phenomenon. But this fact was hidden from us, even from those who knew a great deal about modern European cultural history. I mention this because it is as good an example as any of the absence from our self-understanding of the kind of *relatedness* which makes a people's reality intelligible in terms of the wider cultural, historical and—in the Irish case— ecclesiastical context to which it belongs.

In the first place, we were not generally aware that at a certain stage of our history our manner of viewing reality had *become* fragmented and abstract, or indeed that it had suffered change at all. We did not talk about ourselves or our history in that manner, we had no consciousness of having gone through fundamental changes in our manner of existing and seeing and believing : we were always Irish, we were always Catholic, and these were seen as fixed realities—which they were not.

Secondly, even when we were aware that such and such a cultural or social development had taken place in Europe or in the United Kingdom in the nineteenth century, even when we were well-acquainted with the classic patterns of European, including British, cultural, social and religious history, or at least well-versed in the patterns and vocabularies of analysis through which this history had been seen, we did not attempt to 'read' our own past or present reality in relationship to all of this. We did not test, adapt and modify those discerned patterns of experience and those analytical vocabularies to produce a view of ourselves which would reveal our specific modality within the whole. Such a view would have established relationships of similarity and contrast either in our variant of the common analytical languages or in a new analytical language that would reinterpret the shared experience from our point of view. But such a view of our reality we have not had.

What I have said of fragmentation of vision and of abstraction could be said of liberalism, proletarization, puritanism, the Victorian middle-class ethic, the decline in church art, scientism, positivism, utilitarianism, ultramontanism, the displacement of the Mass by popular devotions, the depopulation of the countrysides, the European messianism of the early twentieth century. Even when we saw and named all these things in a non-Irish context, we suffered from an inability to recognize them by the same names where they occurred in our own lives. Or else—but this was rarer—when we recognized them, we still managed somehow to believe that they were peculiar to us.

I do not speak of that late analysis of contemporary European experience which has stressed the boredom, the alienation, the sense of meaninglessness and absurdity of man in our times. All these were present massively in Ireland; it is no accident that Joyce and Beckett were Dublinmen. But the analysis which revealed these symptoms hardly penetrated the British armour against awareness, and was ignored by the official Catholic Church. Small wonder, then, that we failed to identify them in our own lives : it was a general rule of our self-understanding that things not recognized or countenanced by Englishmen or by the Catholic clergy could not exist in Irish life.

I am talking about the Catholic Ireland I knew in my youth and early manhood and about the kind of self-understanding which permeated life there, colouring our view both of our own reality and of the surrounding world. I speak of it in the past tense because, as I said, the mind of Catholic Ireland is now in a certain state of flux and its new form, if it is to be new, has not yet been revealed. But the mental set I am describing is still very much a reality; it is typified by the newspapers and by the academic establishments, in such cases always the last to change. And so far it has not been challenged in any coherent way; it has been neither replaced nor subjected to systematic criticism and correction.

One aspect of the condition I am describing—the failure to see Irish reality in relationship to a wider context—is sometimes referred to in terms of 'insularity', 'isolation from Europe' or 'from the outside world'. But these metaphors approach the truth only if the 'insularity' in question is seen as a mental insulation from the European and world dimensions of *Irish life*, and from *man in Ireland* : the perfect image in physical terms would be an island shaped like Ireland, and containing our minds, floating above the actual Ireland in the air. It was a variant of that 'severance of mind from world, soul from circumstance, human inwardness from external condition', which Hegel saw as characterizing the alienated European mind.

In the nineteenth century, when we definitively abandoned our own language and became immersed in the insular culture of

G

contemporary England, we lost the sense of belonging to Europe and of sharing in the general condition of man. Within the British insularity of view, we developed—by reaction and by imitation— a second, Irish insularity, defensively excluding from our consciousness most of our involvement in Britishness : Irish nationalist ideology required this. But London and its affiliated Anglo-Saxon establishments, on both sides of the Atlantic, reinforced this idea of Irish apartness and radical difference—both on 'Irish' and on 'Catholic' grounds : by insisting on it and taking it for granted as something obvious, they persuaded us to do the same. Then again, our mental isolation from history and world was being fortified by the isolationist or separatist mentality of contemporary Catholicism. The net result was that, on 'Irish' grounds, on 'Catholic' grounds, and by reason of our provincial-minded relationship to the dominant Anglo-Saxon view, we evolved a general view of ourselves which was in fact an illusion.

Our illusory view of ourselves was, then, the simultaneous product of two ideological convictions, two basic ways of seeing : we believed that our reality was to be perceived in a set of unconnected abstractions, and we believed it consisted of two, mysteriously related *absolute realities*—'Ireland' and 'the Church' or 'Irishness' and 'Catholicism'—each of which separated us radically from the world and man.

An absolute reality excludes relativity by definition. It is something outside history and humanity, and thus mysterious through and through. It is singular, *sui generis*, the only one of its species. It has a single determining principle, and it is only in terms of that principle that it can be analysed. That principle, moreover, is fixed and immutable in nature, so that the reality it determines cannot change. It is the kind of principle which we find assumed both in racialist ideology and in the quasi-religious ideology which sees Absolute Idea or Absolute Justice as the factor totally determining a people's life. In our case, two fixed, essentially related principles were seen as determining our life : Irishness, understood in a racialist manner, and Catholicism, understood as membership of a Church which was Absolute Idea and Absolute Justice combined.

The people of Israel in the Old Testament were seen as an

absolute reality until modern biblical criticism began to relate them to man and to the world of which they formed part, stripping layer after layer of what had been regarded previously as inviolable mystery, learning to see them and to speak of them as men. Our view of ourselves was akin to that old view of Israel. Just as there had been Israel and 'the nations', there was (Catholic) Ireland and 'the world', radically distinct from (Catholic) Ireland and set over against it. Mankind and modern man were 'out there', not 'here'. Even today a phrase like 'the Church in the contemporary world' is not generally felt by Irish people to refer to the Church in Ireland. The actual understanding of the word *world* by their audience is a problem that has not really been tackled at all by preachers of the Gospel in Ireland.

Our view of ourselves as two absolute realities was derived simultaneously from two sources : on the one hand, from quasi-religious English nationalism (English Shinto), with its implicit racialism; on the other hand, from the late Tridentine ideology of Roman Catholicism, which saw the Church (read 'Catholicism') as Absolute Idea and Absolute Justice radically determining the faithful and separating them from world and man. Our absolutism was a fusion in our own terms of elements received from these two absolutisms, the most powerful and extreme of their kind in the nineteenth century. As understood by us, each of the principles which immutably defined us was unintelligible and unmeasurable in general human terms. Given this self-view, our reality defied analysis or intelligibility in terms of contemporary Europe, human history or culture, the contemporary world or contemporary Roman Catholicism with all its actual uniformity and variety.

According to the person or the occasion, either of our determining principles could be seen as predominant. Viewed from our 'Irish' aspect, our Catholicism, like everything else about us, was seen as a function of Irishness, as the religion and morality of this radically unique race of beings. Viewed from our 'Catholic' aspect, *Irish* was a way of describing what a Catholic most truly was. Broadly speaking, the 'Irish' manner of viewing the whole was typically 'lay', the 'Catholic' manner typically clerical, or rather, clericalist. In fact, however, these two ways of viewing our total reality coexisted in most individuals, the one or the other predominating according to whether at a given moment one's Irishness or one's Catholicism was uppermost in one's consciousness. The duality in question was similar to that of race and religion in the consciousness of Jews—and indeed in the general view of Jews by others.

For some of us, though not for the world at large, the connotation of 'Irish' has expanded to include non-Catholic Irish, but usually only by mental addition, as it were, to the basic assumption. One notices how the newspapers, in their critical analyses of maladies described as 'Irish', deal exclusively with Catholics, *their* institutions and *their* clergy. In recent years, and specifically in the public criticism of our Catholicism during the Council years, this 'lay' view of our absolute Irish/Catholic reality has predominated : our Catholicism has been seen largely as a function of our Irishness, its characteristics as peculiar to Ireland and thus as essentially attributable to blood, genes, 'national mind and character'—in a word to 'race' rather than Rome. (The Dutch Catholics' view of their maladies was precisely the opposite.) Since many of these critics thought they were thinking and viewing in a new, untraditional way, their racialist, isolationist assumptions are a good example of how deeply the absolutist mental set affects our manner of seeing.

Our ideology of unconnected abstractions within an absolutist framework must have had advantages or served necessities, otherwise it would not have been held on to so firmly for so long. For one thing, obviously, it buttressed our claim to separate identity and therefore to nationhood. But it was also the source of grievous troubles for the lively, more than ordinarily intelligent people who made up the absolute reality. In the first place, you could not really know about the human group to which you belonged and which defined you. I mean in the ordinary sense of knowing, which is what matters for purposes of living : 'knowing' as men can know a workmate or a brother, a town or a car. Secondly, you could not relate your own reality intelligibly to the surrounding reality so as to gain an adequately intelligible view of your world as a whole. Thirdly, and following from these, you could not evaluate your people, yourself or your situation intellectually.

You could only *feel* that you and they were so or so or *believe* the evaluations of you and yours given by some 'them up there' or some 'them over there' who possessed power over your life and who spoke with certainty and authority : Catholic clergy, Protestant Ascendancy, Englishmen, 'native Americans', nationalist leaders.

So we suffered from an actual ignorance about ourselves and about our relationship to the surrounding world, though our ideology made us believe that we *knew* how these matters stood. We suffered from a submerged crisis of identity and from the consequences thereof in our lives; for our lives could not wait for the missing knowledge that they needed, they had to go on.

Ignorant, in fact, of what it meant to be *us* and *one of us*, each of us was deeply insecure about where he stood in the general scheme of things, how he ranked as himself among others. So, like a young girl who repeatedly consults her mirror and the looks and remarks of men, trying to determine her self and her rating by having them determined for her, we listened with avidity to what others had to say about us, especially our only near and very powerful neighbour, England—the rugby type next door with the flashy sportscar!—and encouraged them to go on talking, to say more. Or, to change the simile, we were like people whose insecurity and hunger for status, or fear of losing status, make them all ears for 'what the neighbours will say' or 'are saying'.

Even today, leader writers and television talkers, bishops and curates, know that they will drive their point home if they threaten or allege the disapproval of 'the world' or of 'foreign observers' for a course of action which they wish to decry. 'The reputation we have' for this or that, 'the shame it is (or will be) for Ireland'—these are potent motivations influencing action, making principles waver, bludgeoning moral freedom and independent thought. People are not laughed at when they suggest we should reform our musical education or change our censorship laws in order to 'improve our image abroad'. Many of us, even men with minds trained in academic disciplines, have got so used to looking 'elsewhere' for general evaluation of themselves as people, of their lives and their acts, that they have long ago mistaken the mirror-image for their own countenance. They no longer notice, as they write or as they speak, the impulsive glance over their shoulder that is a substitute for independent exploration and assessment of their reality in collaboration with their fellow Irishmen and fellow Catholics.

Our inability to analyse and relate our reality intellectually leaves us completely at sea when in fact we attempt to relate, as we are doing all the time. How often have we not heard that infantile division of reality into 'here in Ireland' and 'elsewhere', as if the variety of the world were simply dual! The 'elsewhere' is usually a mental blur. For it is not only before Ireland and our own reality that our minds shy : they balk equally at the other component peoples of Ireland and at foreign peoples; they balk, in short, at the surrounding reality too. We have moved around the world, we have written, but we have written hardly any travel books, and the lack of historical or cultural studies of foreign peoples by Catholic Irishmen is total. In the sphere of general judgments and statements about our world as a whole we have been so utterly at sea that, except during the seminal period of our revolution, we have had nothing to say that was of any real consequence either about ourselves or about man and the world in our time. Our relationship to the general discourse of the age has at best been that of unimaginative commentarists. What is 'here', we say, is better or worse than what is 'elsewhere', it is the best in the world or the worst; that it is radically different is assumed. Usually that 'elsewhere' is nowhere and serves a merely emotional purpose. For some, whose awareness of the surrounding reality has at least attained to a fixed provincial-mindedness, it is London and its cultural environs or—for theologians especially—'the Continent'.

Since the characteristics I am describing have run right through Irish Catholic life, affecting mentality and mental set in regions which the schooling system and academic studies did not touch, much less change, real intellectual activity was impossible. Real intellectual activity is always a grappling with reality, in one or other of its aspects, by a person who has a related, articulated view of reality as a whole, including himself and his people as

an element within it. Adequate general views of the whole, and of
the various aspects of the whole, are prerequisites. In our case,
such intellectual activity has been barred in advance by ideological premises and ways of 'seeing' which precluded adequate
general views.

It is terrible for a people to live from father to son, for several
generations, without an intellectually-founded view of itself in the
context of man, world and peoples, for it to have to rely for its
evaluation of itself and its situation on feelings, faith in others and
hearsay; this is terrible in the sense of terrifying. It is profoundly
disheartening, in such circumstances, to have to accept on faith
that human nature this side of death is a pitfall of sin that leads to
hell's pit eternally, extremely depressing to hear as the predominant opinion of the great surrounding civilization, with which one
shares a common language, that one's people, by reason of their
blood and their religion, are a subhuman and benighted species.
Paddy the Irishman in *Punch* had a monkey's features. Add to
this the course of events in several centuries of Irish Catholic
history—not so terrible in itself as in the fact that it seemed to
confirm the curse which our ancestors were already believing to
be the inheritance of humanity in general, but of themselves and
their country in particular. Already—as a late Tridentine church-
people—a 'guilt society', they became a 'shame society' too,
through immersion in the Victorian middle-class culture and
value-system; the combination was ego-shattering. True, the
Church gave strength and encouragement of a kind, but these
were seen as concerned with an 'elsewhere' in the remote future,
not with here and now. Priest-politicians, land-war agitators,
nationalist leaders and prophets spoke momentarily heartening
words, but the feeling of self-worth they offered was usually related only to the remote past and nothing they said or did seemed
to change the basic situation radically. Then, too, there have
always been some of our own whose self-hatred led them to collaborate wholesale with the alien depressors, their bitter, discouraging words helping to promote the development of a discouraging
environment.

Our evaluation of our absolute reality could result in a feeling that our condition was either positive or negative *absolutely*—that it was 'all' or 'nothing'. Our most persistent feeling has been the latter—that it was 'nothing'. Our view of ourselves as reality at all was being constantly undermined by the feeling that we were not *really* real, and that reality proper and life's centre was 'out there', 'over there', 'elsewhere', where 'the world' and mankind, modern man and the saints were. So we inclined to the feeling that Ireland and our Catholic/Irish selves, were, for this world's purposes, 'nothing'. Being Irish/Catholic was still sensed as an absolute state, even as an absolute 'reality', but of a negative, not *really* real kind, as non-being rather than being—as mere existence.

This led to a gnawing anguish, to an irrational, despairing hatred of our existence here and now and thus of 'Ireland' and 'life in Ireland' and the fact of being 'Irish', words all of them that stood for 'our existence here and now' or for 'the given circumstances of our existence'. Our confidence broken, we sensed no promise or salvation 'here', no possibility of *being* 'here', only of existing. For all sorts of reasons that seemed to lend objective support to a view of ourselves-in-Ireland as a 'situation without promise', but on the deepest level out of a metaphysical *Angst* in regard to our present state which we explained to ourselves in terms of 'being Irish' and 'of Ireland', we placed our hope 'elsewhere', hoped for our salvation 'elsewhere'. For all of us, more or less, 'elsewhere' was purgatory, where we hoped to arrive after death as 'holy souls' and hopeful sufferers. But millions in the meantime saw their saving 'elsewhere' in geographical terms and sought it in America, Britain or Australia. There, in those places of promise, you could 'make something of yourself', could 'come to something'.

As for those who stayed in Ireland, they generally managed to come to terms with their anguish in various ways and for most of the time : where there are status and material security to win and hold against odds, charity and compassion, good companionship and prayer, acceptance of God's inscrutable will to buttress you, despair cannot merely be lived with—it can be put beyond the reach of consciousness. You grumbled habitually about the powers that controlled your world—weather, government, bishops,

employers, 'the educational system'; you surmised the worst in
everything and everyone; you twisted facts, elaborated fictions
and grasped at straws to confirm to yourself that your plight
was dire, your race intrinsically defective; you formed with your
fellows a society whose public voice was never that of gratitude
or of wholehearted praise and which was therefore a fundament-
ally irreligious society; but, unless you were drunk or too young
to have learned the rules, you avoided getting hysterical about
it and were grimly tolerant. Every European people, even every
class within each people, has had to find its own way in modern
times of living with despair. We found our way, and it was
easier for us than for most; for our despair was not of the absolute
kind—there was always purgatory to look forward to.

This view of Irish reality as absolute, fixed and negative
underlay and alternated with a view of the same reality as absolute, fixed and positive (perfectly moral, perfectly Catholic, intrinsically spiritual, uniquely cultured). Much of recent Irish
history is essentially the story of the see-saw relationship between
these two unworldly, inhuman and therefore illusory views. Since
both were in fact rationalizations in nationalist, materialist, religious or racialist terms of enduring value judgments about life
as such, they were not affected—could not be affected—by the
objective facts of the Irish situation or by changes in that situation. The need to find 'objective' confirmation for one's fundamental feeling about life has meant that, for more than a hundred
years now, the same kind of language has been used again and
again to describe the general Irish condition, though the situation has in fact been changing all the time.

The predominance over the past ten years or so of a funda-
mentally negative view of our condition offers as good an example
as any. For the past ten years Ireland has been prospering as never
before; material standards of living have been rising; emigration
has been more than halved; good medical attention and the
higher forms of schooling are becoming available to larger numbers each year; there has been greater political stability than ever
before and the Republic has been taking a more active part than
previously in international affairs. In these years Ireland has in

G*

fact become, relative to population, one of the richest and, objectively speaking, one of the most fortunate countries in the world, providing material amenities that are second to few and standards of public life and of administration of justice that are second to none. Moreover, the present condition of life in Ireland has largely been made possible by the basis which was laid in the previous decades of independence. To name but one fact which points to much else : fifty years ago the death rate in Dublin was, at 27 per 1,000, the highest of any major European city—by the 1950s it had been reduced to 10 per 1,000. Yet the generalizing judgments about the Irish situation which have predominated for the past decade on the public scene were often couched in terms very similar to those used to describe conditions in Ireland in the years of the great famine of 1846-7.

An instance offers itself as I write. In a columnist's daily piece in a national newspaper we read the following :

'Tuairim, I am told, are offering £100 for the best essay on 'The Future of Irish Democracy' and entries must be in before the end of the year. Anyone who wants to draw attention to the distempers of our distressful land by this means may have details from Mrs M.S., etc.'

Perhaps it must be stressed once more, for non-Irish readers, that the journalist is *not* referring to any topical disasters, scandals or the like; he is merely assuming, on good grounds, that essays on a general aspect of Irish affairs will be along the lines he suggests.

Some weeks ago there was the more complex example of the Cork university teach-in. Organized by students belonging to the students' representative body of University College, Cork, it received a great deal of publicity. The subject was 'The State of the Nation'. The leading organizer, interviewed by a newspaper beforehand, spoke of a 'growing lack of faith in a future in Ireland' among the students and said, in regard to the teach-in, that he and his colleagues were 'hoping for an explosion'—a phrase, incidentally, which linked these Cork students with an important strain of modern messianism. The circular advertising the teach-in contained a brief, indirect description of the present state of affairs in the form of questions :

What is happening to Ireland? . . . Can we ever recover the ground we have lost in the last fifty years? How can we make up for the loss of a million of our people and most of our national identity? How can we as students and as future citizens influence public opinion and salvage what we can from the wreck?

Significantly, only one of the eminent speakers at the teach-in—and he spoke from the floor—rebuked the student organizers for this hysterical language, so contradictory of what a university should stand for. But the real point has still to come. Two questions in the circular, which I omitted when citing the text above, actually got to the heart of the matter : they referred to a 'cancer of the soul' and a 'disease' (presumably psychic or mental) which was felt to be afflicting the Irish people. But this true intuition was ignored and not followed up. The organizers were unaware that they themselves were displaying the 'cancer' in action when they allowed their existential pain and their consequent self-hatred to dictate the lunatic view of present Irish reality which they offered to the public. They organized the sessions of their teach-in to deal with the 'aspects of the disease' (as they put it) under the old, hackneyed, fragmented headings of 'Politics', 'Economics', 'Education', 'Culture', 'Religion', etc. and devoted no session to the 'disease' itself, to the inhuman relationships of ideas, mind, feeling and actuality which determine how we 'see' ourselves and our world, while failing in fact to see anything for what it is or ourselves for what we are. The eminent speakers and the press in its comments also ignored the 'cancer of the soul' which had been intuitively sensed by the students—only to be cast aside. So the end state, after this 'talk fest' as after so many others like it, was the same as the first state : we were still enmeshed in the relics of that view of ourselves as an absolute, unrelated, dehumanized and fragmented reality which we inherited from our nineteenth-century ancestors.

Of course, the very existence and force of our mind-paralysing ideology points beyond it to the situation which engendered it. As Erik Erikson, the American authority on identity problems, has said : 'Total defeat breeds a sense of total uniqueness' (he was referring to postwar Germany). The total destruction of our native culture and society at their most developed levels had delivered the people defenceless into the alienating and provincializing totalisms of late Tridentine Roman Catholicism and English politico-cultural imperialism. With ideology taken from these we fashioned our twin, self-alienated uniqueness-illusions. Except at a very undeveloped level in Gaelic, there was no healing core of ancient, indigenous realism to fall back on or to offer challenge. Germany has retained such a core, the vigour of which is perhaps the principal explanation of the continuing ability of the German mind to meet each successive wave of the modern alienating process and answer it with thought rooted deeply in integral human reality. In our case, radical provincialization set in.

Provincialization, as a form of mental alienation, is a feature of European cultural and ecclesiastical history over the past two centuries. Its most extreme developments occurred earliest in France and the English-speaking countries and within the Catholic Church. Catholic Ireland was not unique in its alienation of its secular mind to London : the case has been the same with Irish Protestantism, with the North of England since the First World War, with Scotland and Australia. In a similar manner, the mind of New England has surrendered its functions to New York. Sheer urban bigness plus financial power functioning as the criterion of right thinking and right practice is the intellectual aspect of the concentration and monopolization which we associate with liberal capitalism. The result, for those who come under its spell, is either of two things : an irrational invalidation or—by reaction—overvaluation of life not lived, or of views not held, in the place where most money and the biggest crowds are. It is as if Athens, by dint of looking at the size and wealth of the Persian Empire and the spendours of royal Susa, had lost heart and stopped thinking.

As the secular mind alienates itself towards the biggest, the richest, the most powerful concentration, the alienation of the religious or theological mind is towards the geographical place where the Church or theology is believed essentially to be. One's own local church, *its* Christian experience and *its* theological insights are invalidated. Rome and 'the Continent', meaning the Catholic regions of Western Europe, including Italy, have been regarded for some time past the place where the Church and theology essentially are. The religiously alienated tend to see their own Christian lives and their own church through 'continental', 'Latin' or 'Italian' eyes—that is to say, not really at all. They are inhibited in regard to locally and personally rooted insight, though locally and personally are in fact the only ways that human insight, properly speaking, can take place.

Provincial-mindedness is unmanning in a man; in a Christian it is that and more—it is a crude form of idolatry. Wherever two or three Christians are together is a centre of the world, and for the two or three it is their world-centre. Provincial-mindedness, by denying this, dismisses Christ and devalues man. When it affects a people as a whole, that people and its individual members are radically dehumanized and lose the sense of having God alive among them.

Catholicism is nothing if it is not the way to Christian maturity. But Christian maturity presupposes mental and moral freedom, intellectual self-possession, a personal grasp on reality achieved in the only place and way that such a grasp can really be achieved: in and through one's immediate, socially and historically determined life-situation. Unless such freedom, self-possession and grasp are already being achieved to a high degree, Christian maturity, which is their fulfilment, cannot develop—has nothing to build on—all the theology and piecemeal reforms emanating from the Second Vatican Council are in vain. Gabriel Vahanian says that 'Christ without culture is just as much a chimera as a Christ of culture', and one can add that Christianity without Culture—without freemen—is a chimera too!

The Christian significance of the Irish revolution lies precisely in this field. Alienation, mental and moral provincial-mindedness, gropingly perceived and grappled with, were its first concerns. Through its entire formative period and beyond—in a man such as Michael Collins—the recovery of moral manhood in Ireland, intellectual and spiritual freedom under God, personal reintegration, were the goals uppermost in the minds of the leading revolutionary spirits. During those years man reappeared in Ire-

land, conjured up by powerful myths. The hidden Christ of
Catholic Ireland was revealed to unperceptive eyes and ears by
Irish Catholics. But the work of analysis and relation, which
might have extracted reality permanently from these myths, was
not done—and has not yet been done. The leading revolutionary
humanists suffered violent death; in the cultural and moral
spheres narrow dogmatists claimed to be their heirs. After that
period, when an enduring intellectual breakthrough into reality
was within our reach, the old mental set resumed its sway in
new forms. The old rhetoric and the old dumbness reigned in
place of living words. Having lost man from sight again, we had
nothing of importance to say about life.

The good practical work that has been done since then by
Irish Catholics at home and abroad was left without a vision to
give it coherent, consciously humanistic purpose. Like all good
works of men done without a vision of man alive, it was done in
a subhuman dusk—which made our humanity itself invisible to
us.

Consider this question of our humanity. The very essence of the
predominant self-view was its failure to see humanity in the
Irish/Catholic context, to see Irish/Catholic life as human life.
Yet the fact of the matter is that, measured by the ancient tests
which the discernment of species and the language itself have
given to us, Irish Catholic life has not merely displayed obviously
human and humane qualities : in all important respects but one,
it has been human and has displayed humanity to a noticeably
high degree by the standards of contemporary culture. It is worth
examining this 'unconscious humanism'.

The ability to turn inwards in reflection, ordering the world's
disparate phenomena and one's own relationship to them through
the process of thought, is the decisively humanizing ability inherent in human nature. Ortega y Gassett, in his essay 'Presence-
in-self and Alienation', contrasts this human potency of reflective
inwardness with the condition of animals, even apes, condemned
to a perpetual outwardness and to continual reaction to external
phenomena. *This* quality of humanity has been missing from
Irish life, hence our inability to see and think generally, our

incapacity in the making of general judgments and evaluations of our world and of ourselves in relationship to it.

But there is another quality of mind—the effective use of reason in the sphere of particular perceptions, evaluations and decisions—which also ranks as a specifically *human* faculty. Measure, that most humane quality of life, derives from it. Rooted in common sense, it holds men back from frenzy and deliberate cruelty, seeks to be humane according to its lights, works with intuition in the discernment of persons and the assessment of concrete situations. Shared by a people, it moderates social relations and the exercise of power, brooks potential or existing antagonisms. It ensures the safety of air travel and the efficient distribution of post. This quality of particularized realism and effective good sense has, on the whole, been a mark of Irish Catholic life, in its civil, ecclesiastical and personal spheres, for quite some time past.

An armed revolution and the establishment of a new state are a supreme test for this faculty. We stood the test well. No more gentle revolution in its economy of violence and in its treatment of people than the Irish one. No new state that has abused power less or treated the supporters of the former enemy more kindly. Though the revolutionary ideology seemed to suggest that we should prohibit emigration with its consequent 'contaminations', ideology was in fact ignored and this fundamental human right respected.

The Vatican Council and its sequel in the Church have been another test. The Council took us by surprise, discussion has been vigorous, our relationship to religion and our consciousness of the Church have changed greatly in a few years. But we have not split into warring factions calling each other names. Our journals concerned with church affairs have not taken to denigrating or sneering at this or that section of the Church in Ireland, much less the Catholic life and practice of any other country. Our editors would not countenance it nor would we stand for it. Indeed, hysterical, aggressive writing is generally absent from our quality journals of any kind and from our contemporary literature. The verbal cults of sadism, homosexuality and violence, the high-pitched inquisitorial tones, which masquerade as 'intellectual' expression in New York and London have no bridge-head worth mentioning in our society.

In short, *humanity*, understood as clemency in the exercise of power, restraint in the use of violence, compassionate concern for people and for the fellowman, has characterized Irish Catholic life in its dark period, making government benevolent and human relations relatively gracious. But *humanity*, used qualitatively, has a second meaning, and there is also a special meaning of *human* which corresponds to it.

Wherever, in English-speaking countries during the past century or so, the Anglo-Saxon brand of *Herrenvolk* ideology was weak or at least not operative and the Irish were encountered and known in person-to-person contact, people have remarked on how *human* they were, have been struck by their *humanity*. Indeed, partly through modern Irish literature in translation and through the writings of Ireland-admirers, the opinion that the Irish are 'very *human* people' has penetrated Germany and Northern Europe, thus becoming an accepted commonplace in the post-Protestant countries generally. In this case humanity means spontaneity, charm and warmth—the qualities most noticeably lacking in corpses.

That being human should have acquired this special meaning is an interesting comment on the contemporary culture. That Irish Catholics should be so characterized indicates, in effect, that they have been more impervious than their neighbours to the death-like influences of that culture. They are seen as possessing 'life'—in relative abundance.

The dusk which has prevented us from recognizing the abundant and obvious elements of humanity in our lives together is the half-light in which men live when they lack reflective, integrating inwardness. No hope of taking cognizance of even this elementary 'fact' about our shared life when we were not given to seeking within ourselves for ordered knowledge of ourselves in relationship to man and world. While our humanity, such as it was, lacked this decisely humanizing element, *man* in his Irish Catholic milieu was not realized in us. Our ideological self-view, once taken for granted, became a barrier to the exploration of ourselves in relationship to man and humanity, since it appeared to settle the question of identity (non-humanly) and excluded relationship by its absolutism. Thus reflective inwardness, and with it the possibility of *realizing* our humanity—in the very act of taking cognizance of our *broken* humanity—were rendered impossible by the very nature of our self-view.

Our lives went on there, while we led them in the illusory light of a fiction that was not there. Men were not made, nor was man made in us, because not knowing ourselves as the makings of man and men nor caring to make either, we could not become either.

Proletarians, as Arnold Toynbee points out, are not made by being in a subordinate condition, but by living in a society of which they do not feel themselves to be organically active members, with the rights due to them. In the eighteenth century we became such Hebrews in Egypt.

As contemporary men, we belonged to the rising *undercurrent* of European modernity, its proletarian stream—tending, as the Hebrews did, towards 'existentialist' interpretations of life. But we were caught up, through our immersion in British middle-class culture and late Tridentine Catholicism, in the mentality of the *overcurrent*, the 'liberal bourgeois' and 'abstractionist' stream.

As we wandered into that desert of soul, our country became deserted of people. When we needed to know that we suffered from uprootedness and had lost community, we learned to believe that roots were obstacles to progress and that the nature of man is to be on his own juxtaposed to others. When we needed to know that we found this present life absurd, we learned to believe in 'reasons' that pretended to explain it. Needing to know that we were man and bearers of divine history, we accepted that man and godliness were essentially 'up there' or 'over there' where some 'they' were and that we could acquire humanity or godliness *really* only by assimilating ourselves to some 'them there'. Lacking a philosophical outlet, our existentialist tendency found powerful expression in certain separatist writings and in imaginative literature—the line stretches from Mitchel, Pearse, Joyce and Yeats to O Faoláin and Beckett. *Ulysses*, the warped revelation of a wandering Jew married to an Irish woman, was, in a sense, our unrecognized latterday bible, the dragged up subconscious of what Joyce called his 'race'. (The degree to which it was also the subsconscious of the age has been borne out by a world making *Ulysses* its bible, complete with exegesis and hermeneutics.)

Proletarians need a historically-rooted principle of cohesion and belonging : some of our contemporaries found this in the predestined-class idea, we found it in the fused ideas of church and nation. Proletarians need a promised land before them 'now' that has another promised land, an ideal one, beyond it, 'later' : some saw these as the proletarian state and eventual communism, we saw them as an Irish state and eventual heaven.

Because a church that attached us indirectly to God was part of the collective idea that enabled us to see ourselves as belonging together here and as sharing in a common destiny hereafter, our salvation mode excluded conscious atheism by its formal premisses. Stretched on the rack between proletarian actuality and liberal, abstractionist mentality, we managed to blaze a trail through modernity that made the incarnate God suffer negation in us while yet enduring as commanding and consoling Spirit. However ambiguously, the *fact* of our enduring faith-in-the-dark controverted the standardized 'modern man' both of the liberal capitalist overcurrent and of atheistic proletarianism and existentialism.

At the centre of our supposedly seen, but actually unseen life, was our actual life and our actual humanity unrealized, while we were in continual flight outwards from that centre—by way of our minds, by way of our disintegrating society and cultural community, and by way of a massive physical migration to great cities, mostly abroad, where we expressed our strangeness to ourselves and our loss of self and reality by 'losing ourselves' in a crowd of strangers in strange surroundings. At the centre of our lives—for we gathered regularly in his name and he keeps his promises—was life himself, man absolutized and God-related, Jesus Christ, buttressing and feeding our unconscious humanism, giving us life as abundantly as we allowed. But he was not seen by us either for what he was or where he was : we saw him as a holy ghost and apart from us. Thus he remained perforce—perforce of our inhumanly darkened minds—our full and fullest life unrealized in us.

Blind to man in us, we were blind to our divinity as well. We sensed that the divine presence had departed from life, so we called our everyday activities and our public affairs 'secular', meaning distinct from 'religion'—from our relationship with our life-departed God. Sensing that God had died here, we dressed his priests in black, sang dirges instead of hymns, put our religion into mourning, spoke dead language, not living words. But the absence we were mourning was our own absence from ourselves —our mental exile from our actual embodiment in history, world and man. God's Easter was still valid; but for men who would not be men its effectiveness was cramped. It was we who needed our own, specifically *human* Easter rising—and minds that would recognize it when it announced itself with 'noise in the street'.

A few years ago I knew none of these things. I began to think seriously about our condition and circumstances during the period of violent public criticism of 'Irish Catholicism' which accompanied the early and middle parts of the Vatican Council. My thinking was further stimulated by the celebration of the fiftieth anniversary of 1916 and by the reading it induced me to do.

The criticism occasioned by the Council and by the conciliar movement generally attacked many aspects of our religious and moral life, from the rosary to the bishops, from sexual attitudes and morality to the schools system and welfare services. At its most resonant it was conducted by lay people who believed that the things they saw wrong were, at least in the extreme degree of their wrongness, specifically Irish phenomena. The implication was that they were caused by 'Irishness'. The term 'Irish Catholicism' and the phrase 'here in Ireland' were constantly on the lips of the critics.

I had lived for years in various parts of continental Europe and had travelled in Asia and America. While I had not been a specially keen observer of religious phenomena, I had kept my eyes open. As I heard this or that feature of life in Ireland decried as specifically *Irish*, often to the accompaniment of comparisons with how things were 'elsewhere', I found myself asking mentally again and again, with incredulity at first—'But don't they know?' When the ignorant statements were not contradicted or corrected, when I saw that there was no opposite tendency with a wider, more informed view, setting Irish phenomena in a general Catholic and contemporary focus, I became fascinated. I saw that there was more to the criticism than met the eye, that this excited, bitter talk was an unconscious expression of some underlying ideology, some state of mind and soul, some painful relationship to self.

While the wave of complaint was at its height, I went to Freiburg in south-west Germany to work as assistant to the editor of *Herder Correspondence*. I remember discovering how much I had been indoctrinated, despite my resistance, by the campaign at home when I entered Freiburg Minster for the first time and **was momentarily** *surprised* to see a poster for a Lourdes pilgrimage on display and a magazine called *Fatima Messenger* lying on a table beside a rack filled with the German equivalent of CTS pamphlets. I was caught out again by a slight reaction of surprise when I saw people—it was the end of May—going to May devotions in a parish church, and again a few weeks later when the sermon at Mass was on devotion to the Sacred Heart. So far had the myth-making gone at home that a wide range of popular devotions, which had originated in the Latin countries of Europe in modern times and established themselves in Ireland in the last couple of centuries, were widely regarded as peculiar to Irish Catholicism.

Another side to this myth-making had made Germany, because of the lead it had given in theology, liturgical reform and reformed catechetics, into the dreamland of Catholic discontents. Bishops were gentle there, were all progressive theologians; clergy and people were as one; profoundly intellectual young Catholics with deeply personal Christian convictions were streaming from the schools; priest and people offered Mass together, singing, answering and acting as a true people of God; Catholics and Protestants fraternized in Christian amity, admiring each other's faith. Of course, in fairness to Irish Catholics, I should say that this myth was general at that time throughout English-speaking Catholicism.

Already as a student in Bonn and living for nearly a year in Cologne I had got to know and admire many features of German

Catholicism. But in my two years in Freiburg, forced to compare
the reality around me with the unfounded assumptions in a great
variety of Catholic journals from English-speaking countries, I
acquired a more balanced and critical view both of the German
situation and of the respective strengths and weaknesses of Catholic life and practice in its various contemporary manifestations.

The new catechetics, introduced years before in the German
schools, was not producing a new generation of profoundly convinced Christians—less and less young people were practising
Catholics. When Bavarian countryfolk migrated to Munich, it
was more usual for them to stop practising their religion than it
was for Irish Catholics who migrated to England. In the ordinary
parish the liturgical reforms had not resulted in revitalized worship; the usual impression at Mass in a German city was of
people being deadly earnest, very formal, rather mournful and
a shade self-righteous about themselves and their performance
before God. German intellectualism was splendid at the top, but
on its second and third levels it was often life-frustrating jargon.
Theological get-togethers apart, the in-fighting of Catholics and
Protestants in local politics, public institutions and social life was
of a degree such as I had never heard of or experienced in
Dublin.

Life in the city I lived in was said to be dominated by the
archbishop. There was a current phrase about him 'peeping
through every keyhole'. The pubs closed at twelve o'clock midnight, an hour earlier than in most of the larger German cities;
people said, 'At midnight, the archbishop creeps through the beer-
pipes'. A letter from his office could reprove a department-store
for an allegedly indecent window display or could make one of
the local night-clubs remove the displayed photos of its dancing-
girls.

I was not appalled by these things. On the one hand, I understood them in the light of human nature, German culture and
modern Church history. On the other hand, I knew that these
were the kind of things which the Vatican Council was trying to
change or reform or put an end to. The German contribution to
the Council was tremendous. Such observations merely helped me

to understand why the desire for change had been so very intense and urgent in Germany.

An important thing which I now became increasingly aware of was that our Catholicism at home was not 'traditional' in any real sense, though this adjective was constantly being used to contrast it with the 'progressive' Catholicism of 'the Continent'. Previously, in Spain, Italy, Germany and elsewhere I had got to know really traditional Catholicism. I now realized that my first close contact with it had not been in Ireland growing up, but when I went as a student to the Rhineland. I noticed in the regions around Freiburg how the cult of the ancient local saints, including several Irish saints, flourished as it had not done in most of Ireland even in my grandfather's time. I saw the shrines in the fields, the religious images in the pubs. I became aware of the venerable dignity of cathedral chapters. And of course the sheer material survivals of the Catholic past in cathedrals, churches, church art, abbeys and so on could make you cry as an Irish Catholic.

At home there were people calling our faith and practice 'peasant Catholicism', but of course it was nothing of the kind. Unfortunately for our culture and for life in rural areas, our peasant Catholicism had been destroyed in the nineteenth century. You could find such Catholicism still in Germany, Italy, Spain, France and Poland, and with it a more humanly fulfilling life in many rural areas than you could find in the culturally denuded Irish countryside.

Most important of all, I came to see this rootedness of German Catholicism in centuries of continuous culture as one of the principal reasons why it had of late shown such 'progressive' vitality in many fields. One of the principal causes of the German theological renaissance, I suspected, was the continuing presence in Germany during the ultramontane period of older and different theological traditions. The door to the past had been kept open and out of that past was now coming the new theology. I saw that the existence of old faculties of theology in the German universities had played an important role by providing an alternative institutional base besides the seminary system— to some degree an underground theological stream distinct from

the 'seminary theology' which had been our only theological
resource in the English-speaking countries.

In short, we had suffered not merely from having the late
modern brand of Roman Catholicism, which everyone else had
too and which was theologically anaemic : we had suffered even
more from having *only* that—from having a theology and practice which were *merely modern*, lacking in a sense of history, not
rooted in a religious and cultural past. In this sense, our Catholicism had suffered not from Irishness, but from an 'American' or
'Australian' history-starvation.

When the Council ended, the storm of criticism which it had
whipped up in Ireland died down. In many spheres of church
life, work inspired by the Council went on; but no systematic,
constructive critique either of our church life or of our political
life or of both together, developed. I now see that the outburst
of excited criticism was sterile for three reasons. Firstly, unlike
the fruitful critiques made, say, in France, Germany and Holland, our critique did not concern itself, by and large, with the
Church as Church : it was concerned with local church phenomena seen not as manifestations of the contemporary Catholic
Church (which they were), but as Irish peculiarities. Secondly,
our critique did not concern itself with culture and cultural
history—thus involving of necessity a critique of modern Anglo-
Saxon and European culture. It saw the Church as existing alongside culture, not as conditioned by culture through and through
(which it is). Thirdly, our critique did not concern itself with
the actuality of Irish Catholic life and history seen as an organic
whole (which it is) but with a capricious abstraction from our
actual lives termed 'Irish Catholicism'.

As a result of these mistakes in identification, our critique at
its loudest and most resonant was directed against a fictional
entity. Small wonder, then, that it withered away into piecemeal
reformist ventures, complaints and clichés.

When, over a year ago, my good friend and colleague Herbert
Auhofer, founding editor of *Herder Correspondence*, was killed
in a car crash, I succeeded him as editor in Dublin. Since then
my working life has been bound up almost exclusively with this

journal, the English-speaking sister, so to speak, of the prestigious German *Herder-Korrespondenz*, which played a leading role during the 1950s in preparing the way for the Second Vatican.

Editing *Herder Correspondence* from Dublin has meant more to me than an editor's job. I am glad to have been building a bridge—with this journal of German origin and in collaboration with continental European colleagues—across the mental gulf that has hindered our creative involvement in Europe since we lost the Irish language and acquired a national seminary at Maynooth. Since a like mental gulf has impoverished thought and life in all the English-speaking countries, I am glad that *Herder Correspondence* is an international journal, circulating throughout the entire English-speaking world : this gives to its bridge-building efforts their fullest possible dimension.

My work with *Herder* has taught me some things about Dublin and Ireland. It is a sober journal, eschewing ideology and avoiding shrillness. Pursuing such a policy has been easy in Dublin : despite rumours to the contrary, it is a sober city. But *Herder Correspondence* is also a rather outspoken journal and its theology has tended to be 'progressive'. Editing it here has brought home to me how tolerant Dublin is towards new ideas.

In the first months people would ask me apprehensively, 'What has the Archbishop got to say?' The truthful answer was that I did not know, since I had never met him nor heard from him.

When, on a visit to Freiburg, the veteran editor of *Herder-Korrespondenz*, Karlheinz Schmidthüs, asked me 'What do the bishops say?', and I answered 'I'm going to disappoint you, but I don't know, they have never communicated with me', and he said 'That piece by the Dutch theologian in your last issue, we wouldn't have published it in *Herder-Korrespondenz*—the bishops are taking more interest than ever in us'—I thought for a moment that I had discovered something about our present situation in Ireland. I reflected a bit and said, 'I think we have become un-shockable. After all, none of your bishops has been called a "moron" on German television. Almost everything has been said in Ireland these last few years. The impact of the Council was sharper than in Germany.'

That was true, but I was thinking other thoughts as well. I was remembering that our state censorship, even in its frenzied years, had never banned philosophical, theological or political writings —had never banned *ideas*. And I was wondering, not for the first time, were we simply impervious to ideas, good, bad or indifferent, and had our rulers sensed this and felt no danger in letting us read—and discuss, of course, but only discuss—every latest near-heresy or revolutionary theory from that 'outside world' which we took not a whit more seriously than we took ourselves—and that was not really seriously at all, despite some deceptive appearances to the contrary.

Dublin teaches you that tolerance of ideas can be a very ambiguous value. It can mask despair, superficiality or a frivolous approach to life. It can be the most extreme insult possible to philosophy, an insult which the Greek cities in their heyday never gave.

Only once in about twelve years of active journalism in Dublin, writing in all sorts of publications and doing work on radio and television, did I suffer 'clerical censorship'—and that was in an article I wrote on Zen Buddhism! I did, however, in all media, run into the censorships, pressures and exclusions, some of them purely editorial, some of them commercial or governmental in origin, which are to be expected in a capital city. On such occasions, when my immediate irritation had passed, I would sometimes feel consoled. At least they still care, I would think, at least it's not all indifference and flabbiness, words and thoughts still matter! For it is a good while now since I became aware that no period of culture we call great has coincided with a time or a place in which anyone could say or publish anything he liked, without let or hindrance.

A few years ago a Yugoslav university lecturer, Mihailo Mihailov, returned from a visit to the Soviet Union and wrote an essay 'Russian Summer' which landed him in jail. His vision of the Soviet Union was that, having gone far towards achieving its political and economic revolutions, it was now due for a 'third revolution' in the spiritual and intellectual sphere. In an essay I wrote for the Irish-language journal *Comhar* in December 1965 I applied this diagnosis to the Irish situation, pointing out that for

us this 'third revolution' would really be a return to the central
aim and purpose of the Irish revolution.

In order to achieve this revolution we need to take possession
of ourselves coherently through reflective inwardness and internal
dialogue. We need uninhibited and unified internal dialogue about
what we are, what we know and what we believe. Mihailov went
on to say:

> 'The conflicts which will take place in the future in the Soviet
> Union will have to do with this third revolution . . . they will
> take place primarily in the intellectual sphere, not in the
> economic and social spheres.'

I accept such conflicts, for I see them as necessary concomitants
of a more fully human life than we now have, as birth pangs of
a life-wisdom and a vision which our economic and political life
needs if it is not to be futile. I hope at the same time that we can
keep our conflicts like Unamuno's quarrels with Spain—*querellas
de amor*, lovers' quarrels.

It is not only our lack of seriousness about ourselves that holds
us back from reflective inwardness: our happiness hinders us too.
Perhaps it is a relative happiness, but it is very real as far as it
goes. Edna O'Brien, who now lives and writes in London and
whose very successful novels have been banned in Ireland, once
wrote a film script about her childhood memories of Clare for
British television. She called it *I was Happy Here*. The happiness
she told of was real, we all know it, many who come here revel
in it. But the happiness Edna O'Brien was talking about was a
childhood happiness and I fear that the happiness we know in
Ireland as adults is too akin to that of children to be enough for
adults. One can love the idyll, the gracious pleasures, the sheer
sweetness in Irish life and still want, with St Paul, to be a man and
put 'all childish ways behind me'.

Let me put it this way. That 'possession of our minds and souls'
(to echo Liam Mellows), that achievement of our humanity together, which was the over-riding aim of our revolution requires
entry into self, internal dialogue and internal integration. While
our life remains fragmented and scattered, while we tolerate this,
while we continue to be almost as habitually 'outward-looking' as

apes, we linger in the ante-room of our humanity, homeless and unrealized as men. In this condition, gaping and aping, we deprive Christ of the self-possessed humanity he needs for his incarnation in us, and we belie in the world's eyes (for we call ourselves Christians) his claim to be the completion of man.

Entry into self for self-possession and for possession of Christ is a collective act. Social by nature, a man cannot possess himself alone. Only when the people he is most deeply involved with enjoy a *collective* internal dialogue of all with all, can his reflective inwardness, his internal dialogue as an individual, yield him himself.

At present we lack internal dialogue. In respect of regular channels for exchange of mind and heart, the Irish Catholic church-people are closer to a herd of dumb animals than to a society of men or a living people. We cannot be otherwise while we lack representative assemblies at every level from the parishes upwards. St Paul called the Church of Corinth and the Church at Rome 'the body of Christ', meaning Christ's *living* body. Our Irish Church is more like the corpse of Christ : certainly it is a sleeping body. People of God? Not credibly so. We would first need to become again, as we once were, an articulated and articulate *people*.

True, some parishes here and there are establishing parish councils. But it is only by accident that one hears about them, so few are they and so unpublicized. No better way for frustrating the movement towards assembly at its start and for inducing many parishioners to hold back from what seems an isolated venture and perhaps an eccentricity of their parish priest. Only when it is seen and felt to be a cell in the body of Christ in Ireland—in the Irish Church—will the assembled parish acquire real meaning and purpose theologically and in the average Irishman's consciousness. Coordination, and the sense of purpose and significance which will result from coordination, are necessary if we are to build an assembled church and justify that word *ecclesia* which our present condition belies.

As it happens, such coordination can be provided only by our bishops. Since long before the recent Council they have been constituted as a national conference. All they need to do is to summon the Church in the parishes and dioceses to elect representatives and to assemble stage by stage. Then a national church assembly, with deliberative and consultative functions, could meet in St Patrick's Cathedral at Armagh. The delegates would be chosen by the diocesan assemblies which, in turn, would have been drawn from parish councils based on universal church suffrage. This national or general assembly, which might be given an Irish name, would be convened once or twice yearly by the bishops.

The ultimate reason why we avoid self-confrontation and internal dialogue, both as individuals and as a people, is fear of what we might encounter in ourselves and in our life together. We are afraid there is nothing there but pain. Our recent history, which I have considered in the earlier part of this Postscript, explains how we came to be afraid of life and to inherit this basic fear. But understanding why we are afraid, and why we try to look anywhere and at anything but at ourselves, does not justify our dread. For we believe that Christ is our life and that he is among us and within us. Or at least we say we do. The truth is that his presence among us and in us, by virtue of his promise and our faith, is the definitive reason why an entry into ourselves cannot end in aversion or panic and must lead to a view of ourselves that makes us free and strong. But that view of ourselves, the view that shows God sharing in our identity and us in his, can be ours —not merely as something 'believed in' but as something seen— only if we assemble ourselves, collectively and individually, in internal dialogue. It is when our view comes to comprise in this manner the human and divine elements of our life in one realistic and coherent view that we will find stability in ourselves and the world and feel at home here.

DESMOND FENNELL
Dublin, January 1968

INDEX

221

222 INDEX